WORKING
with
WOMEN'S
GROUPS

Volume

1

Louise Yolton Eberhardt

WORKING *with* WOMEN'S GROUPS

Volume

1

Structured Exercises in:
- Consciousness Raising
- Self-Discovery
- Assertiveness Training

WHOLE PERSON ASSOCIATES
210 W Michigan
Duluth MN 55802-1908
800-247-6789

Library of Congress Cataloging in Publication data 87-50081
ISBN 0-938586-95-5

REPRODUCTION POLICY

Printed in the United States of America

10 9 8 7 6 5 4 3 2 1

WHOLE PERSON ASSOCIATES
210 W Michigan
Duluth MN 55802-1908
800-247-6789

To each of the many women, especially those at the Women's Center of Columbia, Maryland, who have helped create, responded to, and shared in the design of this book through our mutual search for self- and life-affirming choices.

CONTENTS

ASSERTIVENESS TRAINING

RESOURCES

PREFACE

This book had its genesis in the late 1960's when I began to examine with a small group of women the issues of feminism in our lives. We engaged in a mutual exploration of our socialization, attitudes, ideas, and feelings as women in this society. At that time there were few guidelines for such exploration and no resource book of structured designs for facilitating such women's groups. After much experience in working with women around these issues, *Working with Women's Groups, Volume 1,* was written to fill this need.

In the years since this book's beginnings, a great deal has changed; society has changed, women have changed, and I have changed. Great care has been taken to update existing exercises and create new activities to cope with those changes. Many of the revised and new activities stem from ideas offered by women facilitators who have used the previous edition in their workshops. Their help and suggestions have been an invaluable source for updating this book.

I am grateful also to the women I have worked with over the years—all of whom have contributed to the ideas found here—and to all the women and men who have participated in the courses and groups where I developed these exercises.

In this revised volume, I have addressed issues which concern women across the country, including low self-esteem, poor self-image, health problems such as eating disorders and weight concerns, menopause, and empowerment.

This book is designed as a practical guide to share how women can explore these issues. It is written primarily for the facilitator. The goal is to provide you with designs you can easily use, adapt, restructure, and/or expand to suit your particular purpose and group. I wish you success in the use of these exercises and welcome any suggestions, adaptations, or ideas for new exercises. I hope the use of this book will help to enrich the quality of all our lives.

Louise Yolton Eberhardt
Baltimore, Maryland
January, 1994

INTRODUCTION

Many women do not know themselves or their own potential. Bright and capable women, programmed from early childhood for nurturing and subservient roles, are imprisoned by socialization messages. For example, a study by Myra and David Sadker found that, in schools, boys tend to be praised for achievement while girls are praised for interacting well with others. Through our socialization experiences, we internalize and accept to various degrees the message that "women are less than men."

In the late 1970s and in the 1980s, women pushed back career barricades. Younger women today seem to accept these advances as a given and do not want to be identified as feminists. And yet the message to women in our culture is still that no matter what women have achieved, in order to be feminine we must be beautiful and fit an impossible ideal. What women learn at an early age is that physical appearance is primary and they are never all right no matter how they look. And, as most psychologists know, there is a strong relationship between body image and self-esteem.

In response to this socialization process, many women develop a pervasive negative self concept. In women's groups, it becomes clear that the feelings of worthlessness and powerlessness each woman thought hers alone are really symptoms of the cultural stereotypes she has been taught to accept.

In order for women to increase their self-esteem and make more conscious choices about their life focus, it is important to share experiences. Women's groups help many women negotiate transitions from being passive women on the sidelines to assertive and full participants in life. In these groups women can share problems, compare experiences, and explore new options.

Women have learned to play certain roles around men which detract from their learning in a mixed group, so it is important that the group and its facilitators include only women. Mixed groups may discourage women from exploring who they really are as individuals and may reinforce traditional feminine behavior such as playing a listening, supporting role with men, deferring to male opinions and ideas, waiting for men to take the risks, or allowing men to be group leaders. In a group that includes only women, we find joy in growing and changing because it feels right to us, not for male approval.

This book is organized in three different sections: **Consciousness Raising, Self-Discovery,** and **Assertiveness Training**. The exercises, each with a specific set of learning objectives, focus on empowering and challenging women by encouraging personal discovery, growth, and increased self-esteem. A sequence for the exercises is suggested at the beginning of each section.

The book presents structured group experiences that will help women conduct their personal search for identity more productively. In a short period of time women can begin to replace feelings of worthlessness with feelings of value.

Although each of us is unique, because we are women we confront similar obstacles on our journey through life. In women's groups, we can examine the directions we want to take and support each other along the way: women validating women.

Consciousness
Raising

CONSCIOUSNESS RAISING

Consciousness raising is the process of coming to understand sexism and its impact on women and men. Consciousness raising increases the awareness one has about the feelings, behaviors, and experiences surrounding gender roles. At some point in the process, each person experiences an event that produces the "aha," where real personal awareness and insight into sexism and its connection to themselves occurs.

Consciousness raising groups are discussion or "rap" groups where women come together on a regular basis to share their personal experiences with other women, to gain an understanding of their own lives, and to find more positive directions. Learning emerges as the group summarizes and generalizes from each woman's personal experience. Together, group members explore the socialization common to women in this society, uncovering common themes, messages, and oppressions.

The process can be painful at times—anger often surfaces—yet it is also full of joy, excitement, high energy, love, caring, and surprise. Women help women and learn how to support each other. After participating in such groups, women leave stronger, more self-confident, proud of a new-found identity, and often willing to take action against their oppression. These groups were essential to the rebirth of the women's movement during the late 1960s and 1970s and are still relevant today. There is no greater magic than shared support and shared experiences.

Some assumptions underlying consciousness raising groups are:

1. Images, in media and the culture at large, lead to behavior; women become who they are told they should be. For example, women are told what their bodies should look like, that beauty should be a major concern, what occupations they can be in, and what roles to play.

2. Because few women, if any, fit these images or roles, they feel personal dissatisfaction and a lack of self-confidence.

3. Oppression leads to feelings of anger, apathy, and depression. These feelings need to be expressed outwardly so they are not internalized.

4. The socialization and oppression of women leads to women developing internalized sexism—believing many of the negative messages about themselves and feeling that on some level they are inferior to men or "less than men."

©1994 Whole Person Press 210 W Michigan Duluth MN 55802   (800) 247-6789

5. To become conscious of and to articulate alternative messages and images of women leads to women having the freedom to change themselves and—in the long run—society's view of women.

6. In the process of sharing in a community of women, some of the isolation, loneliness and craziness is removed and women learn to support each other and value themselves.

Consciousness raising groups can take a variety of forms and use several techniques, as described in this section. The experiential designs which follow could be used in an on-going consciousness raising group, a classroom (such as a Women's Studies class), or a one time program. Their purpose is to help women look at themselves, to discover how they have internalized their socialization, and to explore new options: becoming more comfortable with themselves and choosing their own futures.

GENERAL COMPONENTS FOR WEEKLY GROUPS

TIME

Two to four hours per session (depending on the activity, the group's limits, and how carefully you watch the clock.)

GROUP SIZE

Any number, but exercises work best with no more than thirty participants. Small groups are often used in the activities, using a facilitator for each group of eight to ten people.

MEETING PLACE/SPACE

In someone's home (suggest changing homes each week) or in a church, school, etc. It is important that the location ensures privacy. A comfortable "living room" space is best.

MATERIALS

Materials needed in each exercise are indicated. Generally you will need one or two easels and easel paper, paper and pencils, magic markers, and masking tape. Worksheets are reproducible, and a set of full-size worksheet masters are available through Whole Person Associates.

©1994 Whole Person Press 210 W Michigan Duluth MN 55802   (800) 247-6789

TOPIC GUIDELINES

It is important to start with low-risk and nonthreatening topics. Start with childhood messages and other socialization exercises then, after two or three sessions, move into more current areas of concerns and then to the more personally threatening exercises. Follow the order below

Early Sessions
1. Childhood Messages
2. Children's Literature
3. Stereotyping in the Media
4. Gender Expectations
5. A Feminist Is

Middle Sessions
6. Ideal Woman
7. Living "Happily Ever After"
8. Feelings About Success
9. Dreams and Hopes
10. Women and Power
11. Cultural Messages and Sex
12. Beauty Standards

Last Sessions
13. Internalized Sexism
14. Women and Aging
15. Attitudes About Menopause
16. Money
17. When I Lose . . . Pounds
18. Women and Competition

In each major grouping above, choose those exercises you want to use. No group will have time, especially in a weekend or even over eight to ten weeks, to cover all the topics. Also adapt each exercise to your specific group.

1 CHILDHOOD MESSAGES

Using open-ended sentences and drawings, participants identify and analyze gender messages and their influence.

GOALS

To identify early messages women received as young girls.

To increase understanding of how messages influence women's self-concept and personal development.

TIME

3 hours

GROUP SIZE

Any number of groups of 8–10 women, with 1 or 2 facilitators in each group.

MATERIALS

Easel and easel pad; magic markers; masking tape; pencils and pens.

PROCESS

Introduction

1. Introduce the exercise with the following chalktalk:
   - As we grew up, we were consciously and unconsciously receiving information about men and women.
   - Today we are going to identify some of these messages and their impact on us all.

2. Form groups of eight to ten women with a facilitator (or two) joining each group. Move to a breakout room or separate space in a large room.

Activity 1: A Good Girl Should and Should Not

1. To break the ice and help the women begin to recall their early messages, take ten to twenty minutes to complete a few of the following open-ended sentences. Using one sentence at a time, ask each person to

take turns completing each sentence. Read out loud or write on an easel the following sentences (or use your own):

- My mother told me a girl should . . .
- My father told me a girl should . . .
- It is most important for girls to . . .
- I was told as a girl I could not . . . and on the other hand boys could . . .
- In conflict situations I was told a good girl should . . .
- Often I got what I wanted by . . .
- When it came to boys I felt . . .
- When it came to other girls I felt . . .
- Teachers and counselors encouraged me to . . .
- I always wanted to . . .
- My mother would almost always . . . and hardly ever . . .
- My father would almost always . . . and hardly ever . . .

2. Debrief the activity by asking the following questions and recording the results on an easel chart:

✔ What were some of the key messages we received as young girls?

✔ What were the messages we received about boys?

✔ What strikes you as the most significant messages, those that had the most impact on your own development?

✔ What feelings do you have about these messages?

Activity 2: Personal Messages

1. Give each person a sheet of easel paper and have various color markers available. Tell them that "we are now going to explore in a deeper way the specific messages we received as young girls."

2. Present the following task:

➤ Consider messages you received about the items listed below while growing up and take ten minutes to draw some pictures that capture their key themes:

➢ Your intelligence, skills and abilities.

➢ Your physical appearance.

➢ Your relationships with others.

➢ Your future.

☞ List the categories on the easel pad.

3. After all have finished, call time and ask each woman to present her drawing to the group, following this process:

   a. Have each woman show her picture and talk about what the drawing represents to her.

   b. Encourage group members to ask questions and share insights from each person's presentation.

   c. Record any new key messages as each woman shares her drawing, adding to the messages previously recorded.

   ☞ *In this process, some women may express deep feelings about the messages they received. It is important to give each woman support and allow adequate time for sharing.*

Concluding Discussion

1. Bring the groups together and ask each group to share insights with the other groups, either through a representative or just impromptu sharing.

2. Direct the group to look for any trends or patterns on the easel chart sheets from Activity 1 and Activity 2.

   ☞ *It is helpful if you tape each sheet up on the wall during a break so all messages are easily seen.*

3. Discuss the following questions:

   ✔ Do we still get some of these messages today? If yes, which ones?

   ✔ Considering the discussion of our drawings, do these messages seem to still influence how you feel about yourself?

   ✔ What would be some healthier messages to give ourselves and our daughters?

VARIATIONS

■ If this is the first exercise with a new group, have participants introduce themselves by sharing what they like most about themselves.

■ Conduct the first activity as a large group (especially if it is a new group), then debrief in small groups.

2 CHILDREN'S LITERATURE

Participants examine the social impact of gender portrayals in children's literature.

GOALS

To examine male/female roles and characteristics in children's books.

To become aware of the influence of stereotypes in children's literature.

To motivate participants to take some action in this area.

TIME

2–3 hours

GROUP SIZE

Small groups of 9 persons, subgroups of 3.

MATERIALS

Easel and easel pads; 30–75 children books (random sample); **Gender Portrayals in Children's Books** worksheet; **Reflection Questions** worksheet; **Action/Interest** worksheet.

PROCESS

Introduction

1. Introduce the topic with the following chalktalk:
   - As children, most of us listened to or read books, unaware of how they impacted us.
   - Many of us now have children of our own, and may not have thought about what messages are conveyed in the stories we read to them.
   - Some of us are or will be educators and need to be aware of what influence the books we use have on children's development.
   - Today, we will examine that influence.
2. Form groups of three; make sure groups are made up of participants who don't know each other well.

3. Give the following instructions:

> ➤ Share what is important to you about gender images in children's literature with the members of your group. You will have ten minutes for your discussion.

4. After about ten minutes, ask for some sample responses from the groups.

Activity 1: Gender Research

1. Ask each person to randomly choose five books from those available and hand out the **Gender Portrayals in Children's Books** worksheets, one for each person and an extra worksheet for each trio.

2. Give them the following instructions:

> ➤ First examine your books individually, using the worksheet to record what you find.

> ➤ When you have each completed this work, share your results with your trio and summarize them on the group worksheet. You will have an hour to complete both of these tasks.

3. After an hour, or when most trios are finished, have each group join two others and discuss their results, recording them on an easel pad using the same categories as the worksheet.

4. Distribute **Reflection Questions** worksheets to each person and ask them to discuss the questions or have a facilitator join each group and ask the following questions:

> ✔ Were male and female characters shown in both traditional and nontraditional roles?

> ✔ Are the achievements of girls and women based on their own initiative and intelligence, or are they due to their beauty or to their relationship with boys and men?

> ✔ Are gender roles incidental or critical to characterization and plot?

> ✔ Are boys and men portrayed in stereotyped ways, i.e., uncaring, unfeeling, in control, as problem solvers, or as warriors?

> ✔ Who is presented as a hero? (males? females? both?)

> ✔ Do women function in passive, supporting, or subservient roles?

> ✔ Do the books show a variety of people from different racial/ethnic and socioeconomic backgrounds? For example, do poor people, people of color, people with disabilities, gay men and lesbians ever

appear in the books and if so, are they shown as happy, successful, and independent characters? Do people of color always play supportive roles?

☞ *The last question above includes diversity dimensions other than gender. This is an excellent opportunity to begin to think about how diverse or homogeneous (white, able-bodied, heterosexual) children's books are.*

5. Ask each group of nine to choose a spokesperson and have them report their research results to the entire group.

Conclusion

1. Have participants return to their small groups to discuss the following questions:

   ✔ What are your feelings about gender stereotypes you may have encountered in children's books? What about any books with non-stereotypical portrayals?

   ✔ What are the possible influences—especially on self-esteem, behavior and future goals—of these books on girls and boys?

   ✔ What were the effects of reading or listening to these kinds of books on your own aspirations and personality formation?

2. Reconvene the large group and ask individuals if they would like to share what they learned through today's experience.

3. The **Action/Interest** worksheet can be distributed, especially if you are interested in forming an action group around this topic.

   ☞ *Before closing the exercise, you may wish to provide some non-sexist examples of books or show the video* **Free to Be . . . You and Me** *(44 minutes) or parts of it to illustrate some alternatives.*

   The video **Free to Be . . . You and Me** *is available in many public libraries. It can also be ordered for about $20 from the Ladyslipper catalog, 800-634-6044.*

VARIATIONS

■ This design could be slightly revised to include children's TV shows and videos, including cartoons. This would usually involve a week-long assignment.

■ Give a brief lecturette on the results of gender studies on children's books and education (works well with college classes).

GENDER PORTRAYALS IN CHILDREN'S LITERATURE

Main Characters (include animals given male or female names or wearing male or female clothing). Put a check under the appropriate column to indicate the gender of the main character. Also indicate what ethnic group they belong to and any other diversity aspects.

Girl   **Boy**   **Adult Male**   **Adult Female**

Gender Descriptions. Record the adjectives or words used to describe the various characters in the books.

Girl   **Boy**   **Adult Male**   **Adult Female**

Gender Roles. Record what the characters are doing and the roles they are performing; i.e. leader or follower, fighting, watching, etc.

Girl   **Boy**   **Adult Male**   **Adult Female**

Gender Occupations. Record the occupations of the characters.

Girl   **Boy**   **Adult Male**   **Adult Female**

Significant quotations about male/female characters:

Other observations regarding diversity:

REFLECTION QUESTIONS

1. Were male and female characters shown in both traditional and nontraditional roles?

2. Are the achievements of girls and women based on their own initiative and intelligence or are they due to their beauty or to their relationship with boys and men?

3. Are gender roles incidental or critical to characterization and plot?

4. Are boys and men portrayed in stereotyped ways, i.e., uncaring, unfeeling, in control, problem solvers, warriors?

5. Which gender is presented as the hero?

6. Do women function in passive, supportive, or subservient roles?

7. Do the books show a variety of people from racial/ethnic and socio-economic backgrounds? (For example, do poor people, people of color, people with disabilities, gay men and lesbians ever appear in the books and if so, are they shown as happy, successful, and independent characters? Do people of color always play minor roles?)

ACTION / INTEREST

As a result of this session, I am (check one)

❏ Bored with the whole topic.

❏ Disinterested because _____

_____

_____

❏ Interested, but don't have time to work on changing things.

❏ Concerned and will do something about the books my children read.

❏ Motivated to do something and would be willing to attend one meeting to discuss some actions we could take. My name and phone number are:

     Name _____

     Phone _____

©1994 Whole Person Press 210 W Michigan Duluth MN 55802   (800) 247-6789

3 STEREOTYPING IN THE MEDIA

By creating collages of gender images in advertisements, the group explores messages about women in the media.

GOALS

To become aware of the male and female roles and images that are portrayed in the media, especially in advertisements.

To identify the gender messages received from the media.

To understand how the media impacts the development of women.

TIME

2 hours

GROUP SIZE

Total group of any number divided into small groups of 6–8 participants.

MATERIALS

A variety of men's and women's magazines; glue; scissors; easel; paper; magic markers; masking tape.

PROCESS

Introduction

1. Present the following chalktalk:
   - The media plays a key role in our lives today.
   - This exercise examines how advertising plays a part in our lives.
   - We will also discuss other forms of media and the messages about gender roles we receive from them.
2. Form small groups of six to eight participants.

Activity 1: Media

1. Equally distribute the magazines to the small groups and give each group a tube of glue, a scissors, an easel pad, markers, and tape.

---

2. Give them the following assignment:

   ➤ Go through the magazines and cut out advertisements featuring men or women.

   ➤ Examine the ads and place them in categories such as sex objects, superwoman, superman, violence to women, unintelligent, submissive and dependent, concerned about appearance, career oriented, positive and equal roles.

   ➤ Make a collage of each category chosen. You may also want to make notes about the topics of the articles in the magazines for men and those for women—noting any differences or similarities—as well as themes and patterns.

3. Give the groups about an hour for the above activity.

4. When the groups are finished, ask each group for their categories and hang similar categories together on the walls.

5. Tell the participants to move about the room, examining the collages and identifying the messages they receive while looking at them.

6. After all have had time to look at the collages, ask for each group to report any themes they may have identified.

7. Return to the small groups to discuss the messages and have participants (or a facilitator) record the messages on a flipchart.

Activity 2: Impact of the Media

1. Reassemble the group and present a lecturette about media images from such sources as Susan Faludi's *Backlash*, especially Part 2, and Naomi Wolf's *Beauty Myth*, especially the "Culture" chapter.

   ☞ *To punctuate your lecture, tape and show gender images from TV ads, music videos, or movies that illustrate current gender images of women.*

2. Conclude by having each woman identify the impact on themselves of these media messages.

VARIATIONS

■ Instead of a lecturette in Activity 2, show the video **Still Killing Us Softly** (thirty-two minutes). The video is available in some libraries or can be ordered from Cambridge Documentary Films, P.O. Box 385, Cambridge, MA 02135, 617-354-3677.

4 GENDER EXPECTATIONS

By imagining their lives if they had been born male, participants examine how gender expectations influence personal goals and relationships.

GOALS

To identify society's expectations of men and women.

To better understand how these expectations influence personal goals.

To help participants clarify their expectations of themselves and of men.

To determine healthier expectations for both genders.

TIME

2 hours

GROUP SIZE

Small groups of 8–10.

MATERIALS

Easel and easel pads; magic markers; masking tape; **Gender Expectations** worksheet.

PROCESS

Activity 1: Cultural Expectations

1. Introduce the topic and goals.

2. Distribute the worksheet and give the following instructions:

   ➤ In the left hand column make a list of what is expected of you because you are a woman; in the right hand column list what would be expected if you were a man. You will have about five minutes for this task.

3. After four minutes, give a one minute warning, then end the writing. Ask participants to form small groups of eight to ten members.

4. Tell each group to discuss the expectations they listed for women and men, making sure to record the items on the easel paper. This is not a

consensus task; all items should be recorded. Ask them to record the women's expectations on one sheet and the men's on another.

5. Have individual groups report their lists to the other groups, starting with the expectations of women.

6. Discuss with the group what differences or similarities they notice between the expectations of women and those of men.

Activity 2: Our Expectations

1. Move back into the small groups and ask participants to reflect on their own expectations, using these questions:

   ✔ Looking at the women's list, are there any expectations you have for yourself? What are they? How do you feel about having and trying to meet these expectations?

   ✔ On the men's list, are there any expectations that you have for men? What are they? What are your feelings about having these expectations? Do men you know fulfill these expectations? How do you feel when they don't?

   ✔ Where did you get your role expectations of yourself and of men?

   ✔ Do the expectations of women influence your goals in life? If so, how?

   ✔ If you were a man, do you think you would have different goals for yourself? If yes, what would they be?

2. Have participants form pairs and discuss what "shoulds" or expectations of themselves and other women they would like to eliminate and what positive expectations they would like to replace them with.

   ☞ *For a variation, have participants discuss which of the men's "shoulds" they would like to eliminate and which positive, healthier expectations they could replace those "shoulds" with.*

Conclusion

1. Reconvene the group and invite pairs to share the "shoulds" they want to eliminate.

2. Conclude by having them voice feelings generated by this session.

GENDER EXPECTATIONS

Expectations of Women	Expectations of Men

5 A FEMINIST IS

This involving activity invites participants to explore their feelings and thoughts about feminism.

GOALS

To explore feminism and define what it means to women and men.

To help participants become clearer about how they feel about feminism and being called a feminist.

TIME

1 hour

GROUP SIZE

Any number of participants, small groups of 7–8.

MATERIALS

Paper and pencils; signs (prepared ahead of time on easel paper); magic markers (dark colors).

PROCESS

Introduction

1. Start with the following chalktalk:
   - Many women have been reluctant to identify themselves as feminists or align themselves with feminism.
   - Today we'd like to explore why this is and gain a better understanding of what feminism is about.
2. Ask the women to raise their hands if they consider themselves a feminist. Count the number of hands and ask them to remember this number.

Activity 1: What Is Feminism?

1. Have the following signs prepared ahead of time and hanging on the wall, covered up:

- A feminist is someone who is . . .
- Feminism stands for . . .
- Present-day feminists (name them) . . .
- Feminists in "Herstory" were (name them) . . .
- Fears/concerns about identifying as a feminist are . . .
- Men's reactions to feminists and feminism are . . .

2. Distribute paper and pencils and tell the participants they are going to explore what feminism is.

3. Reveal one sign at a time and ask participants to write down their responses to each.

4. Then ask them to stand up and use a magic marker to write down their responses on the easel sign sheets. Tell them not to write a response if it has already been written, but instead to check off the response so the group will know how many women had that same thought.

5. When all have finished writing on the sign sheets, reconvene the group. Ask different participants to take a sign and read off what is on that particular sheet.

6. Form small groups of seven to eight participants, moving each group to a part of the room where they can still see the sign sheets. Ask them to discuss the responses on the signs, using these questions as guidelines:

   ✔ What are your personal reactions to what we have put under each category?

   ✔ What trends or patterns are evident?

   ✔ How aare feminists or feminism defined in TV stories, letters to the editor, commentaries in books and magazines, jokes, etc. (e.g., a feminist is unfeminine, not attractive to men, has trouble with sex and relating to men).

   ✔ Have you publically identified yourself as a feminist? What were the reactions you got? How did you feel about this? Or have you avoided identifying yourself as a feminist with others? What contributes to your wanting to be quiet?

   ✔ Can a man be a feminist? If so, how?

   ✔ Have you ever personally known anyone who considered herself or himself a feminist? What were they like?

   ✔ Has feminism or the feminist movement improved your life or made it worse?

☞ *Some key concerns about identifying with feminism you may*
want to cover (if not raised during this discussion) include:

- *Fear of opposing men when men are sexists.*
- *Wanting equal rights for self, but not for all women.*
- *Association of feminism with lesbianism.*
- *Racism in feminist movements and how feminism has not*
  often included women of color.
- *Feminism is only about women.*

Conclusions

1. Ask each woman to say where she now stands in terms of feminism and being identified as a feminist.

2. If the number of women identifying themselves as feminists has increased, make appropriate comments about this.

3. End with this quote by Rebecca West:
   - "I myself have never been able to find out precisely what feminism is: I only know that people call me a feminist whenever I express sentiments that differentiate me from a doormat."*

VARIATIONS

■ Show a video on the history of women or feminism, such as the Ms. Foundation's **She's Nobody's Baby: American Women in the 20th Century** (Your local library should have some current videos.)

■ Give a lecturette or invite a guest speaker to talk about feminism.

*Rebecca West, The Clarion, Nov. 14, 1913, cited in Cheris Kramarae and Paula
A. Treichler, A Feminist Dictionary (London: Pandora Press, 1985) p. 160.

6 IDEAL WOMAN

Individuals share their vision of an ideal woman as dictated by society. Then, as a group, participants develop a picture of the "ideal woman/identified woman."

GOALS

To identify what our culture says is an ideal woman.

To explore how the vision of the ideal woman applies to each woman.

To examine the impact of these images on each woman's image.

TIME

2 hours

GROUP SIZE

Any number of small groups of 8–10 participants.

MATERIALS

Easel and easel pads; magic markers; masking tape; pencils; **Ideal Woman and You** worksheet.

PROCESS

Activity 1: Ideal Women

1. Present the topic and share the goals of the exercise.

2. Distribute the worksheet and read the instructions.

3. Give participants about three to five minutes to individually write and then ask them to check off the items that describe them personally.

4. When most are done, ask them to choose a partner—someone they do not know well—and then ask each pair to join another pair.

5. Direct the participants to share their lists with each other. Tell them they have twenty minutes for sharing, about five minutes per person.

6. Have the groups of four join another group and facilitator.

©1994 Whole Person Press 210 W Michigan Duluth MN 55802   (800) 247-6789

7. Have the facilitator lead a discussion using these questions:

   ✔ What were your feelings as you discussed the ideal woman with others?

   ✔ In what ways were your lists similar or different?

   ✔ What roles for women did you identify? What are supposed to be the traits or characteristics of women in each of these roles? Are there good and bad roles for women?

   ☞ *Make sure you cover such roles as mother, wife, sex object, or playmate and record these roles and the traits under each.*

   ✔ How close did each of you come to the ideal woman? How does the ideal woman fit or apply to your own ethnic, racial, and class background? How do you feel about that?

   ☞ *The ideal is usually white European/Anglo Saxon which means for women of color the standards are even further removed from reality. For example, a white playmate may be sexually naughty, but a black playmate is a woman without morals, without limits.*

   ✔ What effects do these stereotypes of the ideal have on you?

Activity 2: Women Identified Woman

1. Tape together four or five easel sheets of paper for each group and give one to each group with the following directions:

   ➤ Using words and pictures, create the ideal woman from your perspective, not society's. In other words, create a feminist identified ideal woman. You have twenty minutes for this task.

2. After twenty minutes, call time and ask each group to discuss their creation with the rest of the groups.

3. Discuss the differences between society's woman (male identified woman) and female identified woman. Explore how this new ideal could positively impact each of them.

IDEAL WOMAN AND YOU

Instructions: Identify and list the key roles of the "ideal" woman in our society. Then describe the physical, mental, personality, and other characteristics of the ideal woman in that role.

Roles:	Characteristics:

7 LIVING "HAPPILY EVER AFTER"

Participants examine the promises our culture makes about marriage along with the reality of some marriages and compare advantages and disadvantages of marriage for both genders.

GOALS

To study the advantages and disadvantages of marriage.

To identify the promises and disillusionments of marriage for women.

To better understand the messages women receive about marriage and divorce.

TIME

3 hours

GROUP SIZE

Small groups of 6–8.

MATERIALS

Easel and easel pad; magic markers; masking tape; pencils; **Advantages and Disadvantages of Marriage** worksheet.

PROCESS

Activity 1: Promises and Disillusionment

1. Introduce the exercise and state its goals, then make the following point:

   ● Today marriages, families and relationships are changing dramatically. Yet the theme of living "happily ever after" still exists in many of our minds, even when we have experienced divorce.

2. Give participants the following task:

   ➤ In your small groups, identify the messages our culture gives us about marriage and the promises our culture makes to women. (i.e., men will support us.) Record these messages on an easel chart.

3. After they have listed the promises, ask them to identify disillusionments they have learned through personal experience about the reality

of marriage (e.g., now women have two jobs—in the home and outside the home; women abandoned by men must support themselves and their children with no financial help.) Ask them to record the disillusionments as well.

4. Have the groups first report the promises and then discuss the major themes in these promises.

5. Then have the groups report the disillusionments and discuss what this means for women.

Activity 2: Advantages and Disadvantages of Marriage

1. Distribute the **Advantages and Disadvantages of Marriage** worksheet and instruct participants to fill it out.

2. At the end of five minutes, give a one minute warning, and after six minutes stop the writing.

3. Form small groups of six to eight participants and have each member read what she wrote under each category. One person should record the responses on an easel chart, prepared ahead of time like the worksheet. (They do not all have to agree to what goes on the chart.)

4. After fifteen minutes, ask the group to explore the points on their easel chart. The following questions may be used to stimulate discussion:

   ✔ Do you see differences or similarities in the advantages for men and women?

   ✔ Do you see differences or similarities in the disadvantages for men and women?

   ✔ What are your feelings about what you see on the charts?

   ✔ Based on the chart, are there any conclusions you can make about marriage for men and women?

      ☞ *Usually it becomes clear that marriage has more advantages for men than women.*

   ✔ In light of your conclusions, what are the reasons that men and women get married? Divorced?

   ✔ How does this fit your own personal reasons for getting, or not getting, married? Or getting divorced?

4. Invite members to share what they gained from this experience.

   ☞ *You can use this same process to examine the advantages and disadvantages of having children or being divorced.*

ADVANTAGES AND DISADVANTAGES OF MARRIAGE
FOR MEN AND WOMEN

WOMEN	
ADVANTAGES	DISADVANTAGES

MEN	
ADVANTAGES	DISADVANTAGES

8 FEELINGS ABOUT SUCCESS

Using an open-ended story, each participant explores what success has meant to her and how it has been operative in her own life.

GOALS

To discover society's messages to women about success.

To define what success means to each woman.

To explore how women deal with the possibility of success.

TIME

2 ½ hours

GROUP SIZE

Any number in the total group, small groups of 8–10 persons.

MATERIALS

Easel and easel pad; magic markers; masking tape; pencils; **Story Completion** worksheet.

PROCESS

Activity 1: Success Story

1. Do not present the goals or subject. Distribute the worksheet.

   ☞ *You may want to change the story completion worksheet to one that is more relevant to a particular group.*

2. Read the directions on the worksheet and tell participants they have five minutes to finish the story.

3. Ask each woman to read her story in the total group (or in small group if the total group is larger than twelve.) Have four pieces of easel paper on the wall with the following headings:

   ● "Fear of Success"

   ● "Glass Ceiling"

   ● "Positive Feelings about Success"

- "Doubts about Femininity"

As the women recall their stories, record the main message of each under the appropriate category.

☞ *If a story does not meet any of these categories, tape another sheet of paper on the wall and record it*

4. After each has had an opportunity, discuss reactions to the categories and the messages.

Activity 2: What Success Means to Me

1. Form small groups of six to eight participants and move to separate rooms or places in a large room.

2. Inform them that each woman now has five to ten minutes to tell what "success" means to her and how it has or has not been operative in her own life. You may want to include the following questions as guidelines:

   ✔ In the past, how did you feel about your intellectual ability? What did you do with these feelings? Is it the same or different in your present life? How?

   ✔ How important is it for you to do well in situations, e.g., career, school, job, volunteer work? Does it depend on the situation? Does it make a difference if you are alone or in a competitive situation, especially with boys or men?

   ✔ What are your fears, if any, regarding success?

   ✔ What are the messages women in our culture receive about being successful? Do you agree or disagree with them?

   ✔ What kinds of job discrimination or barriers have you faced, if you have? Is the glass ceiling something you have experienced in your career?

3. After all have talked, instruct the group to generalize. Record the generalizations on an easel.

4. Have each group report their generalizations to the large group.

5. Form pairs and have partners discuss the following questions:

   ✔ In what ways is it important for me to be successful in my own life (using my own definition of success)?

   ✔ Do I want to be more successful? In what ways?

©1994 Whole Person Press 210 W Michigan Duluth MN 55802   (800) 247-6789

    ✔ What barriers am I likely to encounter and how can I overcome them?

    ✔ What kinds of support will I need? What specific things do I need to do now? When will I finish each item?

6. To close the exercise, give an opportunity to those who wish to tell the group how they intend to be more successful or to report any conclusions they've made about success in their own lives.

VARIATION

■ In Activity 1, change the **Story Completion** worksheet to fit the particular group you are working with, i.e., nurses: "As a second-year medical student, Jane—who had been a nurse for five years—finds herself at the top of her medical school class."

STORY COMPLETION

Directions: Use the space below to complete the following story:

After eight years in a major law firm, Susan finds herself being considered seriously for partnership . . .

9 DREAMS AND HOPES

A guided fantasy takes participants through their life, providing time for them to reflect on their dreams and hopes and how they may have changed.

GOALS

To rediscover childhood and adolescent dreams women have had about their futures.

To examine present hopes for each woman's life.

To compare who and where each woman is now to what her dreams were for the future.

TIME

2 hours

GROUP SIZE

Any number in the total group for Activity 1; groups of 10 for Activity 2.

MATERIALS

Easel charts and easels; magic markers; tape; pencils; **Dreams and Hopes** worksheet.

PROCESS

Introduction

1. Give a chalktalk about the reasons for exploring our past and present dreams about ourselves, such as:

   ● We all have dreams of who we want to be or goals we want to accomplish in our lives.

   ● Some of us realize our dreams, others do not.

   ● We usually don't achieve our dreams unless we are willing to express and identify them to ourselves and share them with others.

2. Share the goals of the exercise.

©1994 Whole Person Press 210 W Michigan Duluth MN 55802   (800) 247-6789

Activity 1: Guided Fantasy

1. Ask each person to find a comfortable place on the floor or in their chair. Tell them that in a minute you will ask them to close their eyes and relax while you guide them through some questions about their dreams and hopes for their lives.

2. Lead participants through the guided fantasy on page 34.

Activity 2: Sharing our Dreams

1. After the reading, distribute the **Dreams and Hopes** worksheet and ask participants to take a few minutes to fill it out.

2. After about five minutes, form small groups with a facilitator in each group. Make sure participants bring their worksheets with them.

3. Give each woman an opportunity to talk about the hopes and dreams she had for her life, what she discovered during the guided fantasy, and what she recorded on her worksheet. Use these questions for discussion:

   ✔ What did teachers, parents, counselors, and peers encourage you to be? How did you respond?

   ✔ How did some of your dreams for yourself differ from your present life? How do you feel about this?

   ✔ If your dreams changed, was it because of choice or pressure from others? Who did you feel was trying to influence you?

   ✔ What would you like to change about your life? How could you start working on this?

4. After each woman has had a turn, invite them to generalize about what they each shared and how these things affect them as women.

Closure

1. Reconvene the large group and have each of the small groups share their insights and generalizations.

2. Close by encouraging each woman to pursue her hopes for her life.

©1994 Whole Person Press 210 W Michigan Duluth MN 55802   (800) 247-6789

HOPES AND DREAMS Guided Fantasy

Close your eyes and relax any tense parts of your body . . .

☞ *Pause*

Now let's go back to your earliest memories of being a child . . . How old are you? . . . Where are you? . . . What kinds of toys are you playing with? . . . What books are being read to you? . . . What kinds of make-believe games do you play? . . . Who do you imagine yourself being: a firefighter, a model, a mommy, a soldier, a doctor, an artist, or what?

☞ *Pause*

Now imagine yourself growing older until you are in grade school . . . What games are you playing now? . . . what fantasies do you have now about what you'd like to be when you grow up? . . . Do your parents and teachers encourage or discourage you from exploring who you want to be?

☞ *Pause*

Continue growing older, focusing on this question: who do you want to be as you go into junior high school? . . . high school? . . . college? . . . Are you encouraged to pursue your dreams and hopes or discouraged and moved into a different direction? . . . What direction does your life take you? . . . Do you still have the same dreams or different ones as you grow older? . . . What new dreams do you have for yourself about who you could be or what you could do?

☞ *Pause*

Return to your present life. . . .

What are your hopes and goals for yourself now? . . .

What would you like to do that you have not yet done? . . .

☞ *Pause*

As you feel ready, open your eyes.

DREAMS AND HOPES

Directions: Write in the space below your dreams and hopes for yourself at different points in your life. When you have finished, take a minute to reflect on any patterns or themes that have led you to where you are in your present life.

PRESCHOOL

ELEMENTARY SCHOOL

JR. HIGH AND SR. HIGH SCHOOL

COLLEGE AND GRADUATE SCHOOL

EARLY ADULT YEARS

MIDDLE ADULT YEARS

LATE ADULT YEARS

10 WOMEN AND POWER

Participants identify situations in which they have felt powerful and powerless and use role-plays to explore ways to empower themselves more effectively.

GOALS

To become aware of situations in which women feel powerful or powerless.

To explore how women can empower themselves in powerless situations.

TIME

2 hours (4 if you use the variation for Activity 2)

GROUP SIZE

Any number of participants formed into small groups of 6–8.

MATERIALS

Easel and easel paper; magic markers; masking tape; pencils; paper.

PROCESS

Introduction

1. Welcome the participants and use the following as a chalktalk:

   - For the most part, women in our society have not held much power or control.

   - Because of that, we often experience a sense of powerlessness in certain situations.

   - Today we will identify which situations leave us in a state of powerlessness and explore ways we can empower ourselves in those situations.

2. Form groups of six to eight participants. Assign them meeting space and a facilitator.

©1994 Whole Person Press 210 W Michigan Duluth MN 55802   (800) 247-6789

Activity 1: Power/Powerless Activity

1. Ask group members to think about situations in which they have felt powerful and situations in which they have felt powerless.

2. Ask participants to identify powerless situations and record these on the easel chart, leaving room across from the situation to later record feelings about these situations.

3. When you have exhausted the powerless situations, return to the list and discuss and record feelings women have when they are in that situation.

4. Ask participants to identify situations in which they have felt powerful, or empowered. Record these situations on a separate easel chart, following the same process as above. When all the situations have been identified add the feelings these situations evoke.

5. Reconvene the large group and have a representative from each group present their powerless list, following this procedure:

   a. Ask each representative to read an item and the feelings that go with that situation.

   b. Continue until all situations have been mentioned, making sure to not repeat situations if another group has already said it, even though another group with the same item may want to add some additional remarks about feelings.

6. When all items have been shared, encourage participants to note similarities, differences, and common themes in the situations shared. For example, in some groups, lists of powerless situations may be longer than powerful situations.

Activity 2: Empowering Ourselves

1. Return to the same small groups and explain that participants are now going to have an opportunity to examine how to empower themselves in one of their powerless situations.

2. Give the following assignment:

   ➤ Plan a five minute role-play which will involve two or more of you.

   ➤ The role-play should illustrate how a woman can empower herself in one of the powerless situations the group identified earlier.

   ➤ You will have twenty minutes to develop the role-play. All the role-players should be assigned new names.

©1994 Whole Person Press 210 W Michigan Duluth MN 55802   (800) 247-6789

3. After twenty minutes, reassemble the large group to present the role-plays, following this process:

   a. A group presents its role-play.

   b. A discussion of the role-play follows, beginning by asking those in the role-play to share how they felt in their role.

   c. Ask for responses from the other groups as to what they observed, how the central role-player turned the situation into one in which she empowered herself, and other ways she also might have responded.

   d. Applaud the group's effort and then go to the next group's role-play, following the same process as above.

Closure

1. Ask participants for comments about the role-playing process and what they learned.

2. Form pairs and tell them to discuss how they can and will empower themselves more, identifying what behaviors and/or actions will be necessary.

3. Invite sharing from the pairs and encourage them to work on their empowerment plans over in the next two weeks.

VARIATION

■ For a longer adaptation of Activity 2, reconvene the same small groups and explain that each participant will have an opportunity to role-play a particular situation which she would like to handle more powerfully. Lead the group through the following process:

1. Ask for a volunteer to role-play one of her powerless situations.

2. Then have the woman (Mary) present the powerless situation she wants to work on.

3. Ask her to choose one or more participants to work with her.

4. Move role-players to the center of the group and ask Mary to play the person she is having difficulty with and her partner to play Mary being powerful in that situation.

5. Stop the role-play when there is enough material to explore and ask both of the role-players to discuss their feelings about how they role-played the situation. Then get responses to the role-play and invite other ideas of how Mary can be more powerful in that situation.

6. Ask them to role-play the situation again, this time with Mary playing herself and her partner playing the other person.

7. Again stop the role-play when "Mary" has had an opportunity to practice being empowered and debrief the role-play. First ask the role-players to respond and then invite comments from the group. Be sure to emphasize the positive.

8. Continue the above process with a new volunteer. Conduct the role-plays until everyone has had a chance to role-play one of their "powerless" situations.

Sample Easel Chart

POWERLESS	
SITUATION	FEELINGS
Visit to gynecologist	Child-like, put down
High school mixer	Embarrassed, frustrated
POWERFUL/EMPOWERED	
SITUATION	FEELINGS
Team leader of a work project	Valued, energized
Asserting my rights in a store	Self-respect, exaltation

©1994 Whole Person Press 210 W Michigan Duluth MN 55802   (800) 247-6789

11 CULTURAL MESSAGES AND SEX

Women develop an *esprit de corps* as they recall sexual messages they have received and then develop new, healthier messages to use in their personal lives.

GOALS

To recall the messages women have received about sexuality.

To identify the incongruities which often exist between what we think, what we feel, and what we do.

To determine some healthy sexual messages for ourselves.

TIME

1 ½ hours

GROUP SIZE

Unlimited number of 8–10 member groups.

MATERIALS

Easel and easel pad; magic markers; masking tape.

PROCESS

Activity 1: Identifying Messages

1. Inform the group of the topic and goals.

2. Ask participants to lie down or find a comfortable position and shut their eyes. Tell them to recall messages they received growing up and still get about sex and to say these messages out loud as they think of them.

3. When the energy goes down and the group seems to run out of messages, ask them to stop and open their eyes.

4. Form small groups of eight to ten women and go to a break out room.

5. Have each group discuss and record messages previously identified (and any other sexual messages). Some messages might include:

- Women should be passive sexually. Men should be the aggressors and the initiators.

- Women do not enjoy sex; only endure it.

- A woman is a slut if she has a number of sexual experiences; a man is a stud.

- Men have fragile egos around sex and women should fake orgasms to protect this ego or say sex was great even if it was terrible.

6. Reconvene the large group and have the small groups present their messages by rotating each group's reading of a message until all have been presented.

7. Return to the small groups and ask participants to discuss the following questions:

   ✔ What feelings do you have about these messages?

   ✔ What is the effect of some of these messages on you?

   ✔ What kind of pressure is or was placed on you by others to act on these messages? How do or did you handle this?

   ✔ Are there some messages you intellectually do not believe, but emotionally still accept and act on?

Activity 2: New Messages

1. Ask the small groups to identify new, healthier sexual messages for themselves and other women. List these on a easel chart.

2. Share these healthy sexual messages in the large group.

3. Divide the small groups into pairs to discuss the following questions:

   ✔ What are your feelings about this experience?

   ✔ What are one or two new messages you want to work on giving yourself (e.g., "I would like to act on the healthy message that I can assert myself sexually and initiate sex when I feel like it.")?

4. Provide an opportunity for the small groups to tell the large group the messages they have chosen to work on.

VARIATION

■ If you are short on time, skip *Steps 2* and *3* of Activity 1.

©1994 Whole Person Press 210 W Michigan Duluth MN 55802   (800) 247-6789

12 BEAUTY STANDARDS

This energizing activity explores how societal beauty standards impact women's behavior and self image.

GOALS

To explore societal beauty standards for women.

To examine feelings about these societal standards of women, especially physical appearance.

To realize the impact of these standards on each woman's image and behavior.

TIME

2 hours

GROUP SIZE

Any number of small groups of 8.

MATERIALS

Easel and paper; magic markers; masking tape; pencils and pens; paper.

PROCESS

Activity 1: Exploring Beauty Standards

1. Begin by saying:
   - In this next activity we want to explore how beauty standards have impacted our behavior and self-image.

2. In small groups of eight, lead participants in completing the following open-ended sentences one at a time. After each statement, give each member time to complete the sentence with her own words, then move on to the next statement.
   - If I want to look feminine, I . . .
   - Wearing makeup I feel . . . and if I do not wear makeup I feel . . .
   - Not shaving my under-arms and legs would be/is . . .

- When I see the typical model in a magazine and then look at myself, I feel . . .
- When I see a nude female centerfold, I feel . . .
- Older woman are . . .
- If I'm going to a place where there will be men around, as opposed to all women, I wear . . .
- Dieting for me is . . .
- When the partner I'm with looks at another woman, I . . .
- The part of my body that is most beautiful is . . .
- I would like, am thinking about, or have had cosmetic surgery on my . . . in order to . . .
- If I see wrinkles on my face, I . . .
- When it comes to my weight, I wish . . .
- Exercise to me is . . .
- The amount of money and time I spend on makeup and exercise is . . .

3. In the same groups, discuss this activity using the following questions:

   ✔ How did you feel completing these sentences?

   ✔ What sentence did you have the strongest feelings about? What were your feelings?

      ☞ *For this question it would be helpful to have on an easel sheet the questions or topics used above to help them recall all the areas.*

   ✔ Did you learn anything about yourself as you answered the questions?

   ✔ Where do your judgments of your attractiveness and unattractiveness come from, yourself or others?

   ✔ In general, do you think you are conscious of your appearance more for yourself or for men and/or other women? Have you ever gotten up early in the morning to fix your face before your lover/partner sees you?

   ✔ Do you feel you have any symptoms of addiction to beauty, such as spending huge amounts on cosmetics, always dieting, or spending a large part of each day on your appearance?

   ✔ Are you happy with the amount of emphasis/non-emphasis you are putting on your appearance right now?

©1994 Whole Person Press 210 W Michigan Duluth MN 55802   (800) 247-6789

✔ What societal beauty standards do you buy into but wish you did not? Do you ever feel like our society has stereotyped women to have either beauty-without-intelligence or intelligence-without-beauty? Is there a relationship between standards set for women's beauty and the desire to limit our development as women?

✔ Do you flirt with others to try to reinforce your feelings about yourself? How much of your sense of self-worth comes from your physical appeal?

✔ What standards do you like and wish to keep as your own? How could these standards impact how you see yourself?

✔ What would it be like to be loved for yourself alone, the way you naturally are?

Closure

1. End by inviting persons to share significant things they learned as a result of this experience.

2. Make appropriate closing remarks such as:

   ● The message we receive as women is that we are never okay no matter how we look. We need to begin to accept and love ourselves the way we are.

VARIATION

■ After *Step 1* of the Closure activity, encourage each woman to tell the group what she would look like and what she would wear if she felt free to be her natural self.

13 INTERNALIZED SEXISM

The concept of "internalized sexism" is defined, and each women is given the opportunity to assess her own level of internalized sexism.

GOALS

To understand what internalized sexism is and how it operates in women.

To give each woman an opportunity to identify her internalized sexism.

To explore how to eliminate internalized sexism.

TIME

2 hours

GROUP SIZE

Groups of 8–10 participants.

MATERIALS

Easel and easel pad; magic markers; masking tape;**Internalized Sexism** worksheet.

PROCESS

Activity 1: Ice Breaker

1. Ask each woman to answer this question:

   ✔ What is something that you think is negative about women, a characteristic or trait you think women tend to exhibit that annoys you or you don't like?

2. When everyone has answered, lead a discussion about major themes or patterns in their answers.

3. End the ice breaker with the following points:

   ● Many of our answers were negative messages about how women are gossips, manipulative, whiners, bitchy, etc.

   ● Belief in these negative messages leads us to develop what is called internalized sexism.

©1994 Whole Person Press 210 W Michigan Duluth MN 55802   (800) 247-6789

● Today we are going to explore this concept and examine how it manifests itself in each of us.

Activity 2: Defining Internalized Sexism

1. Give a brief lecturette about internalized sexism, highlighting the following points:

   ➤ Internalized sexism involves buying into society's beliefs and messages about women—that women are inferior to men, that men really are stronger and smarter.

   ➤ It means we participate to some degree in our own oppression.

   ➤ Our socialization helps create a sense of inferiority and incompetence within us as women, which is far more effective than any external controls.

   ➤ Internalized sexism is painful to examine and look at and we are often unaware of it in ourselves and other women.

   ➤ We often internalize that we cannot do a good job without the support of men, leaving us with feelings of inadequacies.

   ➤ Mothers pass on their own internalized sexism to their daughters.

   ➤ Some examples of internalized sexism are:

      ➤ Hating our bodies.

      ➤ Believing that, when a man says something it must be true, but if a woman says the same thing it seems suspect.

      ➤ Not wanting to work for a woman boss.

      ➤ Feeling like you can't trust other women.

      ➤ Blaming ourselves for something that we could not have prevented (such as rape).

2. Ask for other examples from the participants.

3. Invite questions and discussion about internalized sexism.

Activity 3: Internalizing Sexism in Myself

1. Distribute the **Internalized Sexism** worksheet and pencils.

2. Ask each woman to fill out the worksheet, checking off those items she has said or done.

©1994 Whole Person Press 210 W Michigan Duluth MN 55802   (800) 247-6789

3. In small groups with a facilitator, have each woman share what she checked and ask her to give examples of these items. It is important not to be judgmental, but to encourage honesty and openness during this session. Thank the women who are open and honest about their lists.

> ☞ *As the women share, facilitators may want to keep a record on their worksheets of what was checked off. This will help in the next discussion.*

4. When all have shared, lead a discussion with the small group about what they noticed or heard.

   ✔ Are there common items most of us checked off?

   ✔ What personal impact does this kind of thinking have on each of us?

   ✔ About what items would it be easiest to change our ways of thinking? Most difficult to change?

   ✔ What areas do you want to start working on now?

Activity 4: New Thinking/Healthier Beliefs

> ☞ *In ongoing groups, add a feedback session before this activity. Encourage feedback about each woman's internalized sexism as recognized by others in the group.*

1. In the small groups, have participants brainstorm some healthier messages or beliefs they would like to have about women and record them on the easel.

2. Reassemble the large group and have each small group share their healthy list with the others.

3. Add the following items if they are not mentioned:

   ● Do not blame women; unify to create strength; create support systems with other women.

   ● Begin to please yourself and not always others.

   ● Do not be afraid of conflict; see it as necessary.

   ● Understand our own internalized sexism, but do not judge self or other women.

   ● Do not turn anger inward; turn it toward the appropriate target.

   ● Be aware when society projects its fears on us.

4. Make appropriate closing remarks.

INTERNALIZED SEXISM

❑ Finding fault and criticizing other women.

❑ Putting down women leaders.

❑ Mistrusting other women.

❑ Protecting men.

❑ Calling women "girls" or "ladies."

❑ Believing women are not as good as men.

❑ Holding in and not sharing one's opinions, ideas, beliefs.

❑ Seeing oneself as the exception: "I'm not like other women."

❑ Valuing men's opinions more than women's opinions and feeling that a man's approval is worth more than a woman's.

❑ Not supporting other women.

❑ Believing in the negative images about women.

❑ Allowing men to abuse you (verbally or physically).

❑ Trying to become like men in behavior, speech, dress, manners, and interests.

❑ Feeling embarrassed by another woman's behavior: "She gives women a bad name."

❑ Putting men first.

❑ Questioning or blaming onself.

❑ (other?)

❑ (other?)

❑ (other?)

©1994 Whole Person Press 210 W Michigan Duluth MN 55802   (800) 247-6789

14 WOMEN AND AGING

This exercise explains significant stages in women's lives and helps them both understand aging and ways to make it a positive experience.

GOALS

To explore the participants' feelings about growing older.

To understand the American culture's attitudes toward women and aging.

To encourage women to take charge of their own behavior and attitudes about growing older.

TIME

2 ½ hours

GROUP SIZE

Total group of any number, small groups of 6–8 participants.

MATERIALS

Easel and easel pad; magic markers; masking tape; pencils; paper; **Significant Life Stages for Women** worksheet.

PROCESS

Introduction

1. Introduce the topic and goals.

2. Ask each woman to give her name (if a new group) and share her age.

3. Lead a brief discussion of this experience by asking:

   ✔ How did it feel to acknowledge how old you were?

   ✔ Did you want to give another age? Did anyone lie?

   ✔ Do you sometimes avoid sharing your age or lie about it? If you do, under what circumstances?

   ✔ Do you feel flattered if you hear "you don't look your age?"

   ☞ *The implicit message is "You look good because you don't show you're aging."*

©1994 Whole Person Press 210 W Michigan Duluth MN 55802   (800) 247-6789

✔ Were there any surprises when you heard others give their ages? Does this say anything about our images of women at certain ages, how we think they should look or act?

4. End this activity by saying:

● One of the most universal of gender-related beauty standards has to do with age, associating youth in women with beauty. Today the age limit is moving up and yet most of us have many fears about growing older, especially how we will be viewed in terms of attractiveness.

Activity 1: Stages of Life

1. Tell participants they are going to have an opportunity to explore the life stages they have gone through and those they expect to experience. Invite them to think about the following questions:

✔ What have been, and will be, significant ages in your life, especially those ages that will mean some changes in how you live or how others will respond to you?

✔ How do you feel about these changes? Which ones do you dread? Which ones excite you?

2. Distribute the worksheet and ask them to fill it out, highlighting the instructions:

➤ Identify the significant ages for a woman and describe how each age has been or how you imagine it will be for the years you have not yet reached. Focus on the difficulties and the joys you have or may experience at each of the different stages of your life. You have ten minutes for this task.

3. After ten minutes, or when most are done, form small groups of six to eight. Make the groups a heterogenous age mixture.

4. Have a facilitator in each of the groups provide time for each woman to report her significant ages and record them on an easel chart. There will probably be commonality, but record any differences as well.

5. Use the following questions as guidelines for a discussion about the various ages. Start with the youngest age identified and work through each stage with these questions:

✔ What are your actual experiences or imagined fantasies at this age or stage of your life?

©1994 Whole Person Press 210 W Michigan Duluth MN 55802   (800) 247-6789

✔ How do you think it will be for men at the same age? How do you feel about this?

✔ What are some traps women can find themselves in at this age? How could we begin to avoid these traps?

✔ Do the print media, movies, and TV shows portray strong and attractive women at this age? If not, why might this be?

✔ Have you ever experienced ageism in your work during this stage of your life? If so, what was it like?

✔ Have you ever had a relationship where a man left you to be with or marry a younger woman? How did you respond?

Closure

1. Reconvene the entire group and present a provocative idea about women and aging, connecting it to what they discussed in their groups, such as:

   ➤ With age comes authority. Are beauty standards that idealize youth a way of getting rid of women just as they are attaining real power?

2. With all the participants, go around the circle completing the following two open-ended questions:

   ✔ Right now, my feelings about growing older are . . .

   ✔ One thing I would like to do differently about growing older is . . .

3. Encourage them to feel good about themselves at each stage of their life.

VARIATIONS

■ If most or all of the women in the group are forty-five years old or older, you may want to allow more time for them to share their experiences as "older women" in our society.

■ With older groups of women, end by having participants share what is good about being older.

SIGNIFICANT LIFE STAGES FOR WOMEN

Instructions: Identify the significant age periods you have experienced in your life so far by writing down the specific age and also identify the stages you think you will be going through as you grow older. In the appropriate column make some notes about difficulties and joys you have or will experience during each stage.

Life Stages/Age	Notes About This Stage

15 ATTITUDES ABOUT MENOPAUSE

By sharing with each other their fears, attitudes, experiences, and questions about menopause, participants are encouraged to view this important issue as a beginning rather than an end.

GOALS

To examine women's fears about the transition of menopause.

To give women an opportunity to talk about their experiences during this transition.

To explore options women have during menopause.

To receive support from other women to help through this period.

TIME

3 hours

GROUP SIZE

Total group up to 20 women. Small groups of 8–10.

☞ *This exercise is especially relevant to women who are in peri-menopause (transition from regular periods to no periods), in menopause, or past it. Although younger women could benefit from discussing this subject with older women, this exercise has been written as a support group to help women through this transition. Without support during this change, many women feel lost.*

MATERIALS

Easel and easel pad; magic markers; masking tape; **Symptoms of Menopause** worksheet.

PROCESS

Introduction

1. Open with some appropriate remarks about the subject, such as:

   ● Menopause may be the last taboo subject for women to discuss and explore.

- It happens to every woman; with menopause there is no choice.
- Menopause is stigmatized in our society where youth is revered.
- Our shame, fears, and misinformation have kept many of us from talking about and exploring a period of life which affects us all.

2. Have each woman share the following:
   - Her age.
   - What meaning menopause has for her.
   - Her feelings when she hears the word menopause or thinks about it.

3. Make any needed comments about their feelings and then say:
   - ➤ Menopause is a major change in women's lives, and yet this significant passage has been very neglected. Today we want to spend some time examining this important transition.

Activity 1: Menophobic

1. Form small groups of eight to ten women and ask them to identify their fears about menopause. Record these on an easel chart.

2. Ask participants to check off their top three or five fears on the chart.

3. When all are finished, discuss the most common fears in the group. Fears most typically mentioned include:
   - Fear of losing sexual attractiveness and sexual desire.
   - Fear of becoming anxious and getting depressed.
   - Fear of bodily changes, such as hot flashes, weight gain, and wrinkles (fear of aging).
   - Fear of becoming jealous of teenage daughters or younger women.
   - Fear of becoming invisible or being seen as worthless in the society.
   - Fear of losing control.

Activity 2: Symptoms and Experience

1. Lead into the activity by saying:
   - As women many of us want to deny the symptoms of menopause.
   - A few of us will have no problems with menopause and a few will become temporarily dysfunctional. The rest of us will experience difficulties that will come and go over the years.
   - In this activity we are going to discuss our symptoms and experiences.

2. Distribute the worksheet and ask each women to check off the symptoms she has had or is having right now. Encourage her to add any others not on the list.

3. When all have finished, ask the women to share what they checked off and discuss their symptoms and experiences. Give adequate time for this discussion.

Activity 3: Hormones or Natural?

1. Break into four subgroups using the following categories:
   - Women who are taking hormones or want to take them.
   - Women who are not taking hormones and believe in a natural method.
   - Women who have done both during this transition.
   - Women who are totally confused and don't know what to do.

2. Have each group move to the center of the room and discuss their decisions and experiences with hormones or without. Start with the confused group of women, then the hormone group, the natural group, and finally the group that has done both. Follow this process:
   a. The group gets in the center facing each other and shares their experiences without interruption from the women on the outside.
   b. There will be one empty chair in the center group and, if someone has a question, they are to go sit in the chair and ask their question. When the question is answered they are to leave.
   c. Allow at least twenty minutes for each group.

3. When all the groups have shared, ask each woman to rejoin her small group. Present them with the following task:
   ➤ On an easel sheet record the risks and benefits of hormone replacement therapy and the risks and benefits of natural methods. You will have thirty minutes for this task.

4. After thirty minutes, have each small group report their findings to the large group.

5. When all groups have shared, have the small groups divide in half and discuss what decisions each individual would like to make about how to deal with the changes in her body.

6. After about fifteen minutes, invite participants to share their decisions with the total group.

7. Encourage the women to continue this discussion with their doctor and
    to read several books on the subject.

    ☞ *The following books are recommended: Susan Lark,* **The Meno-
    pause Self Help Book**; *Lonnie Barbach,* **The Pause**; *Gail Sheehy,*
    The Silent Passage.

Activity 4: A New Beginning

1. Ask each woman to share what it would mean to them to "claim the
    pause" and move into a new period of their life.

2. Have them identify how they can help educate their partner about this
    transition period and the kind of support they will need.

3. End with a discussion of how women can continue to support each other
    during this exciting change in their lives.

VARIATION

■ Invite a woman medical doctor who is well respected and open to all
   options to help the women discuss menopause, especially the use of
   hormones.

■ Ongoing support groups may be formed and agreements to continue to
   meet made.

SYMPTOMS OF MENOPAUSE

❑ Hot flashes

❑ Sleep disturbances

❑ Mental fuzziness—loss of mental acuity, problems with short term memory, an inability to concentrate

❑ Aching joints and muscles—back aches, hip pain, cramping

❑ Gastric upsets

❑ Nausea and dizziness

❑ Headaches

❑ Skin Sensitivities—burning, itching, stinging, or prickly sensations

❑ Heart palpitations

❑ Breast tenderness

❑ Frequent urination or urinary incontinence

❑ Weight gain

❑ Depression or anxiety

❑ Lack of sexual desire

Notes about my symptoms:

16 MONEY

Lively discussion punctuates this exercise as participants share their personal "herstories" surrounding money and examine how it has impacted their relationships.

GOALS

To understand what having money means to each woman.

To explore dreams, issues, and concerns associated with money.

To explore how men react to women and money.

TIME

2 ½ hours

GROUP SIZE

Small groups of 8–10.

MATERIALS

Easel and easel pads; magic markers; masking tape.

PROCESS

Activity 1: Personal "Herstories"

1. Start by asking each woman to share her personal history and first impressions of money, including the value and power of it. Give no more than five minutes per person.

2. Ask each woman to discuss her first memory of earning money and what it meant to her.

Activity 2: Fears and Dreams

1. Have the group members share their fears and concerns surrounding money and record these on an easel sheet.

2. Then have them share their dreams and fantasies about money (what do they think money can buy them?) and record these on the easel.

©1994 Whole Person Press 210 W Michigan Duluth MN 55802 (800) 247-6789

3. Ask participants to examine both lists and identify major themes about their fears and dreams.

4. Finally ask each woman to think about any shocks they received concerning issues of money (e.g., during a divorce) and then to share what it was about.

5. Discuss whether their shocks were tied into their fears and dreams about money.

Activity 3: Money and Relationships with Men

1. Begin by saying:

   ● Let's explore our relationships with men and how they have responded to us when we've had or earned money and when we've had little or no money.

2. Discuss the following questions as a group:

   ✔ Have you ever been or felt financially dependent on a man? How did he respond? How did you feel about yourself?

   ✔ Have you ever stayed in a bad relationship, afraid to leave because of financial issues? What was the result?

   ✔ If you support yourself, how does this feel? Would you ever give it up for a relationship?

   ✔ In this culture, men's status is attached to having money and women's status as "feminine" is endangered by having money. What do you think? Has this been your experience?

   ✔ Has having or earning money, especially more money than a man you're involved with, been intimidating to the man? If so, how? If not, how did he respond?

   ✔ Have you ever tried to hide the amount of money you make from a man? If yes, for what reason?

   ✔ Have you ever given up a job or a career for the sake of a relationship? What was the result?

   ✔ Who controlled the money when you have lived with a man (or have you chosen not to live with a man and this is one of the reasons, to keep your independence and freedom)? Do you pool your money and if so, what is the impact on the relationship?

   ✔ Have you ever been in a relationship where you lived from day to day and counted every penny? What was the impact on the relationship?

✔ Does a man have to earn and have a lot of money for you to be interested or see him as sexy or a potential partner? Why or why not?

3. Ask participants to generalize from the discussion; discuss major themes about women, money, men, and relationships.

Conclusions

1. End by having women in pairs share what this session has meant to them.

2. Invite pairs to share in the large group.

VARIATION

■ For an ice breaker to begin this exercise, ask participants to take money or credit cards out of their wallets and say what it means to them to have them available.

■ If the women have a career or job outside the home, ask the following questions at the end of Activity 1:

✔ How assertive are you around the issue of money? (For example, have you ever changed jobs to make more money or asked for more money?)

✔ Do you wait hoping to be noticed and given a raise? Does waiting work for you?

17 WHEN I LOSE . . . POUNDS

In this engaging exercise, participants explore how our culture impacts women's feelings about their size.

GOALS

To examine women's issues about their weight.

To begin to understand how our culture encourages women to feel they are never thin enough.

To discuss and share experiences with weight loss and weight gain.

TIME

2 hours

GROUP SIZE

Small groups of 8–12 participants

MATERIALS

Easel and easel paper; scale; magic markers; masking tape; **Weight Questionnaire** worksheet.

PROCESS

Activity 1: Ice Breaker

1. Begin with the following statement:
   - Today we are going to examine our issues, feelings, and experiences surrounding weight.

2. One at a time, have each woman to the easel and put a check under the apporopriate column for question 1. Then, have them wiegh themselves and answer the remaining questions.

   ☞ *The easel chart should be prepared ahead of time. The information to place on the chart is found on page 63.*

3. When all have weighed themselves and filled in the chart, lead a discussion of their answers on the easel chart.

©1994 Whole Person Press 210 W Michigan Duluth MN 55802   (800) 247-6789

4. Ask participants:

   ✔ If men had just weighed themselves, would they be feeling the same way as you do?

5. Finally, ask each woman to answer the following open-ended sentences:

   ✔ Fat women are . . .

   ✔ Thin women are . . .

   ✔ When I feel fat I am . . .

   ✔ When I feel thin I am . . .

5. Lead a brief discussion of their responses to these questions.

Activity 2: Weight Questionnaire

1. Distribute the questionnaire and ask the women to fill it out.

2. In small groups, have participants share their answers to each question.

3. Reconvene the large group and ask participants to share what they have learned.

4. Make the following points:

   ● The average today model is twenty-three percent thinner than the average woman. Models were eight percent thinner a generation ago.

   ● On any given day, a high proportion of females—from young girls to adult women—are on a diet.

   ● Women are seen as mature if they starve and immature if they eat heartily.

   ● Our culture does not give women the message that our bodies are fine in any shape or at any weight.

   ● Women who seek to lose weight may be interested in becoming healthy or may be seeking the answers to their problems by trying to be in control of their bodies and appetites.

   ● Healthy men are less concerned with their body image than women are. Most think they are closer to the ideal.

Activity 3: Impact of Concern with Weight

1. Ask each participant to finish this question:

✓ When I lose this weight (or gain this weight) I will . . .

2. Discuss their answers, including personal motives for losing weight (e.g., desire to be popular, loved, successful, acceptable, in control, healthy, etc.)

3. End with the following thought:

● Over concern with our weight leads to poor self-esteem and a low sense of personal effectiveness.

VARIATION

■ To save time, have participants weigh-in as they arrive.

■ Watch either **The Famine Within** or **Eating**, videotapes about issues concerning diet, and discuss them after viewing. **Eating** is a particularly enlightening discussion about women's relationship to food and their weight concerns. Showing this video could make an excellent follow-up session or act as part of a longer workshop.

☞ *The Famine Within, produced by National Film Board of Canada, can be found in many libraries. Eating, a full length movie, can be found in video stores for rent.*

Easel Chart: Weighing In

1. Before weighing yourself, how do you feel about your weight?

Too Heavy   Just Right   Too Thin

2. After weighing yourself, how do you feel about your weight?

Too Heavy   Just Right   Too Thin

3. What is your ideal weight?   What is your actual weight?

©1994 Whole Person Press 210 W Michigan Duluth MN 55802   (800) 247-6789

WEIGHT QUESTIONNAIRE

YES NO

❑ ❑ 1. I can never really enjoy a meal.

❑ ❑ 2. I never feel thin enough.

❑ ❑ 3. I dread summer's approach and the thought of wearing a bathing suit.

❑ ❑ 4. I weigh myself every day or more than once a day.

❑ ❑ 5. I think about food a good part of each day and night.

❑ ❑ 6. I compare myself to the average model in magazines and find myself overweight.

❑ ❑ 7. Dieting off and on has been part of my life.

❑ ❑ 8. I have had (or have) an eating disorder, such as anorexia, compulsive eating, or bulimia.

❑ ❑ 9. My doctor has encouraged me to lose weight.

❑ ❑ 10. Exercise is part of my daily routine.

❑ ❑ 11. I smoke to keep weight off.

❑ ❑ 12. I am afraid to quit smoking for fear I will gain weight.

❑ ❑ 13. I frequently lose control and binge excessively.

❑ ❑ 14. I vomit or take laxatives, diuretics, or diet pills to control my weight.

❑ ❑ 15. I am preoccupied with my body size and body image.

18 WOMEN AND COMPETITION

Group members participate in a "line up" to explore competition among women. (This exercise works best with groups whose members know each other and have worked together for awhile.)

GOALS

To become aware of what participants define as attractive in themselves and in other women.

To begin to understand how competition among women works and its results.

TIME

2 hours

GROUP SIZE

Groups of 8–15

MATERIALS

Easel and easel paper; magic markers; masking tape; pencils; paper; **My Self-Image** worksheet; **Group Ranking** worksheet.

PROCESS

Introduction

1. Introduce the topic with the following chalktalk:
   - Today we are going to explore our attitudes and feelings toward other women. These attitudes often reflect our own feelings about ourselves and our own womanhood.
   - Most of us look around and rank others in comparison to ourselves, especially those of the same gender. Doing this influences how we feel, think, and act, though usually we keep it under the surface and do not talk about it.
   - Today we are going to try to understand what really happens.

2. Distribute **My Self-Image** worksheets and pencils to each participant and give the following directions:

➤ To start we are going to explore how we feel about ourselves. On the paper write three things you feel are attractive about yourself and three things you feel are unattractive about yourself.

☞ *Do not define attractiveness for the group; each woman's definition will vary. It is also important not to discuss this part when they finish, as a discussion might influence Activity 1.*

Activty 1: Line Up

1. Distribute the **Group Ranking** worksheets and ask participants to write down the names of each woman in the group, including themselves, in order of attractiveness (however they are defining it.)

2. When they have completed this task, tell them they are now going to physically line each other up. Pick a volunteer from each group and procede as follows:

   a. Line up each woman across the room, with the first person the most attractive and the last person the least attractive, according to the volunteer's list. The volunteer will also place herself in the line.

   b. When she has finished, have another woman volunteer to change the line-up according to her own criteria.

   c. Continue this procedure until every woman has had an opportunity to line up the group.

   ☞ *This experience may create some intense feelings. A few may be unable to participate. The important thing is to process whatever happens. The "line-up" constantly changes and no one usually remains at the very end or the beginning of the line throughout the activity.*

3. Lead a discussion of what happened, looking at such issues as:

   ✔ How did you define attractiveness? What were your criteria? Were the criteria related to male-definitions of attractiveness?

   ✔ When you listed three attractive and unattractive traits about yourself were there any patterns you noted?

   ☞ *Often unattractive traits listed are physical ones; attractive traits tend to be more evenly distributed among personality and physical factors.*

   ✔ What were your feelings when you ranked yourself with others? Have you ever done this in private? How do these feelings affect your behavior in a meeting, a party, in this group?

✔ How did you feel when others moved you up or down the line?

✔ Would you feel insecure or threatened if a partner of yours (male or female) was attracted to another woman here? What is it about that particular woman that worries you? Does that in any way reflect feelings you have about yourself? What could you do to feel better about yourself in that area?

☞ *If you have women of color and white women in the group, ask the women of color how they would feel if their partner was attracted/interested in a white woman and the white women how they would respond if their partner was interested in a woman of color?*

✔ Physical attractiveness sometimes impacts how women leaders are viewed. If she is seen by us as too pretty, she may be viewed as a threat or rival and often is not taken seriously by men. If she is not viewed as physically attractive, we may fear that if we identify with her, we may also be seen as ugly. All of these dynamics keep the attention off of the women's identification with issues or subject matter. Have you experienced any of these dynamics? Any others?

Closure

1. End by asking groups for insights and observations.

2. If you worked in more than one group, reconvene the large group for closure and invite participants to share insights.

VARIATIONS

■ If your group is larger than fifteen, form subgroups of eight to fifteen participants. Move to separate meeting areas.

☞ *It is helpful if the groups are made up of women who know each other. If the group members are unaquainted, first have them each introduce themselves to the group by sharing their name and something interesting about themselves.*

■ You may want to record each person's line up of the group on a flip chart to aid in reflection and discussion after the activity.

■ To focus on competition in the workplace, use the following process which explores the concept of the "Queen Bee" syndrome:

1. Tell participants that this exercise explores why women discriminate against each other, especially in the workplace.

2. Share some information about the "Queen Bee Syndrome" covering the following points:

- Some educated and successful women feel they must separate themselves from other women and get status from being one of the few women among men.

- They identify with males and reject women.

- These women will not help other women to advance, partly as a desire to protect their own exclusive and privileged position and partly out of their own internalized sexism.

- Some of these women don't reject women, but feel sexism is not real. After all, they have done well enough and are happy being what they are. (Although they may not deep down really feel this way.) Their belief is that women of talent and ability can accomplish anything they want and can overcome any barriers, that women have equal opportunities everywhere.

3. Ask if any of them have ever acted or felt this way or known any queen bees.

4. Discuss the following:

✔ Do you experience competition between women in the workplace? On what basis?

✔ What are some of the results of this competition? (For example, competition between women keeps us from bonding as men do and from uniting around an issue, interest, or agenda. Men may not like each other or be friends, but will work together for a common goal.)

✔ Why do some women have contempt for other women?

✔ Why is sisterhood or support so difficult to achieve between women?

☞ *Women are kept isolated from each other and are not encouraged to come together for themselves. Women are encouraged to compete with each other for men.*

✔ How can we be more supportive of other women and be less competitive?

✔ What are you willing to do to help change how you relate to other women?

5. To end the experience, ask the woman to report what was learned during the session and/or to describe what they are feeling.

©1994 Whole Person Press 210 W Michigan Duluth MN 55802   (800) 247-6789

VARIATION

■ For ongoing groups, try encouraging feedback to those women who have expressed views that fit the "Queen Bee" attitude. Make sure feedback is desired and constructive.

MY SELF IMAGE

My Attractive Characteristics

1.

2.

3.

4.

5.

My Unattractive Characteristics

1.

2.

3.

4.

5.

GROUP RANKING

Instructions: Write down the names of each of the women in your small group in order of attractiveness.

1. _____

2. _____

3. _____

4. _____

5. _____

6. _____

7. _____

8. _____

9. _____

10. _____

11. _____

12. _____

13. _____

14. _____

15. _____

©1994 Whole Person Press 210 W Michigan Duluth MN 55802   (800) 247-6789

Consciousness Raising Reading List

Alexander, Jo, et al.*Women and Aging: An Anthology by Women*. Oregon: Calyx Books, 1986.

Arms, Suzanne. *Immaculate Deception: A New Look at Women and Childbirth in America*. New York: Bantam Books, 1986.

AAUW. *The AAUW Report: How Schools Shortchange Girls*. AAUW Sales Office, P.O. Box 251, Annapolis Junction, Maryland 20701.

Barbach, Lonnie. *The Pause*. New York: Dutton, 1993.

Bernard, Jessie. *The Future of Marriage*. New York: Bantam, 1973.

Boston Women's Health Collective. *The New Our Bodies, Our Selves*. New York: Simon & Schuster, 1992.

Calyx Editorial Collective. *Women and Aging: an Anthology by Women*. Corvallis, Oregon: Calyx Books, 1986.

Chapkis, Wendy. *Beauty Secrets: Women and the Politics of Appearance*. Boston: South End Press, 1986.

Chesler, Phyllis. *Women and Madness*. New York: Harvest, 1989.

Chernin, Kim. *The Obsession: Reflections on the Tyranny of Slenderness*. New York: Harper, 1981.

Cohen, Marcia. *The Sisterhood: The Inside Story of the Women's Movement and the Leaders who Made it Happen*. New York: Ballantine Books, 1988.

Corea, Gena. *Women as Wombs*. San Francisco: Harpers, 1993.

Craft, Christine. *Too Old, Too Ugly, and Not Deferential To Men*. New York: Dell, 1988.

Daly, Mary. *Gyn Ecology*. Boston: Beacon Press, 1990.

Ehrenreick, Barbara and Dierdre English. *For Her Own Good: 150 Years of the Experts' Advice to Women*. New York: Anchor Books, 1979.

Ehrenreick, Barbara. *Witches, Midwives, and Nurse*. Old Westbury, New York: The Feminist Press, 1973.

Faludi, Susan. *Backlash: The Undeclared War Against American Women.* New York: Crown, 1991.

French, Marilyn. *Beyond Power: On Women, Men, and Morals.* New York: Summit Books, 1985.

Freeman, Jo, ed., *Women: A Feminist Perspective.* 4th ed. Mountain View, CA: Mayfield, 1984.

Friedan, Betty. *The Fountain of Age.* New York: Simon and Schuster, 1993.

Gornick, Vivian and Barbara Moran. *Women in Sexist Society.* New York: Basic Books, 1972.

Heintz, Katherine. "An Examination of Sex and Occupational Role Presentations of Female Characters in Children's Picture Books," *Women's Studies in Communication.* 9 (1987): 69 .

Hewlett, Sylvia Ann. *A Lesser Life: The Myth of Women's Liberation In America.* New York: Warner Books, 1987.

Hooks, Bell. *Ain't I A Woman: Black Women and Feminism.* Boston: South End Press, 1981.

———. *Feminist Theory: From Margin to Center.* Boston: South End Press, 1984.

Kano, Susan. *Making Peace with Food.* New York: HarperCollins, 1989.

Lark, Susan. *The Menopause Self Help Book.* Berkeley, CA: Celestial Arts, 1992.

Lerda, Gerda. *The Creation of Feminist Consciousness.* New York: Oxford UP, 1993.

Lott, Bernice. *Women's Lives.* New York: Brooks Cole Publishers, 1994.

McKinnon, Catherine. *Feminism Unmodified.* Cambridge, MA: Harvard UP, 1987.

Moraga, Cherie and Gloria Anzaldua, eds. *This Bridge Called My Back: Writings By Radical Women of Color.* MA: Persephone Press, 1981.

Morgan, Robin. *Sisterhood is Powerful.* New York: Vintage Books, 1970.

Morris, Celia. *Bearing Witness.* Boston: Little Brown, 1994.

Ms. Foundation for Women. *Programmed Neglect: Not Seen, Not Heard.* National Girl's Initiative, 141 Fifth Avenue, Suite 65, New York, NY, 10010.

Orbach, Susie. *Fat is a Feminist Issue.* New York: Berkley Books, 1979.

Pogrebin, Letty Cottin. "Rap Groups," *Ms. Magazine.* March, 1973.

Porcino, Jane. *Growing Older, Getting Better: A Handbook for Women in the Second Half of Life.* Reading, MA: Addison-Wesley, 1983.

Radford, Jill and Diana Russell. *Femicide.* New York: MacMillan, 1992.

Rich, Adrienne. *Of Women Born: Motherhood as Experience and Institution.* New York: W.W. Norton, 1976.

Sadker, Myra and David Sadker. *Failing at Fairness: How America's Schools Cheat Girls.* New York: Charles Scribner's Sons, 1994.

Sheehy, Gail. *Passages.* New York: Dutton, 1975.

——. *The Silent Passage.* New York: Random House, 1992.

Steinem, Gloria. *Outrageous Acts and Everyday Rebellions.* New York: Holt, Rinehart, and Winston, 1983.

Waring, Marilyn. *If Women Counted.* San Francisco: Harpers, 1988.

Wolf, Naomi. *The Beauty Myth.* New York: Anchor Books, 1992.

——. *Fire With Fire.* New York: Random House, 1993.

Zerbe, Kathryn. *The Body Betrayed.* Washington, DC: American Psychiatric Press, Inc., 1993.

Zinsser, Judith. *History and Feminism.* New York: Twayne Publishers, 1993.

Self-Discovery

SELF-DISCOVERY GROUPS

The Consciousness Raising section emphasized understanding the culture's social conditioning and how this socialization impacts women's attitudes, feelings, and behavior. This section focuses primarily on personal growth through discovering and sharing feelings about self and examining personal attitudes, beliefs, and behaviors. The overall goal is to help women change their sense of themselves, their self-image, and their sense of worth, thereby increasing their self-esteem. As their self-confidence increases so do their aspirations; women begin to create new options in their personal goals.

In a self-discovery group a woman can:

- Explore how she views and feels about herself.
- Learn to know what she is feeling and express these feelings and thoughts freely and openly.
- Expand her awareness of others.
- Discover her strengths, talents, and creativity.
- Give and receive feedback about the impact she has on others and vice versa.
- Discover her life goals, desires, and values.
- Develop more meaningful and open relationships with other women.
- Increase her interpersonal skills.
- Experiment with new behavior.

Self-discovery groups provide time for a woman to be herself, apart from her partner, children, or other significant people in her life. As a result of participating in these sessions, women often report a new sense of independence and freedom plus greater self-confidence, self-esteem, and self-respect. Increased awareness moves us to empower ourselves.

STRUCTURE OF SELF-DISCOVERY GROUPS

A self-discovery group works best when planned for a weekend or for weekly meetings over about two months. The ideal weekend experience includes the following elements:

1. A residential setting (to enable women to get away from outside pressures and responsibilities).

2. A schedule such as: dinner on Friday night and an evening session, three sessions Saturday (morning, afternoon, and evening), one session Sunday morning, ending with lunch that day.

3. Enough free time for women to take a walk, take a nap, read, or listen to music (especially some "women's music").

4. As few other people as possible, especially men, at the conference site.

A weekend generally has a powerful impact, but a eight- or ten-week continuing group may provide more long-term support and growth. In the latter format, a two- to three-hour session can be scheduled once a week.

For some women, the decision to attend this type of group constitutes a risk. They may have not gotten much, if any, support from their families or others; in fact they may sometimes encounter hostility, especially from men. Others, engaged in their first group learning experience, feel unsure of what will happen. Consequently, they may be feeling a great deal of anxiety when they come to the weekend or the first session.

For all these reasons, start off the first group sessions with planned activities. As participants begin to feel more comfortable and more able to state what they want to work on, you may choose to loosen the structure. Eventually sessions with no preplanned structure may be in order, letting whatever emerges happen, but only if you have skilled group facilitators.

GROUP STAGES

Certain stages occur in most women's growth groups which, as facilitators, you can help nurture. What follows is a description of these stages, with suggested exercises to choose for use in each stage.

Stage 1: Inclusion and Acceptance

When women first enter the group, they usually do not know what will be expected. They may be silently thinking: Who else is in the group? What do I need to do to be a part of this group? Can I establish my identity here? What will it "cost"? Thus the first exercises should "break the ice," increase comfort, and include some low-risk interactional designs to help participants begin to feel this is a group they can and do belong to. It also helps to present the group with guidelines for how the group will operate; or even better, ask them to develop such guidelines as one of the first tasks (for suggested guidelines, turn to "How to Use This Book," page 176).

©1994 Whole Person Press 210 W Michigan Duluth MN 55802   (800) 247-6789

Exercises appropriate for this stage include:
- 19 Names and Expectations
- 20 How I see Myself
- 21 Who Am I?

Stage 2: Self-Disclosure and Awareness of Self and Others

At this point in the group, the participants are becoming familiar with each other. If a supportive and accepting climate has been built in the first stage, they are more willing to reveal their feelings and thinking (e.g., confusions, self-doubts, hopes, goals, fears).

The focus in this stage is on self: spending time on where each participant is as a person. Discovering perceptions, behavior patterns, and feelings generates excitement. An awareness grows that together they share many similar experiences and feelings. A trusting empathy develops among the women.

Exercises that support this stage are:
- 22 Lies about Myself
- 23 Life Goals
- 24 Dreams and Possibilities
- 33 Strength Bombardment
- 1 Childhood Messages (see the **Consciousness Raising** section)
- 25 Body Awareness
- 27 Sexual Experiences

Stage 3: Group Relationships

Having disclosed a lot during the first two stages, participants now feel more intimate in the group. They are also aware of disparate feelings toward others and are more ready to express these. This does not mean they will readily confront each other with negative feelings or even share affectionate ones easily. A structure will enable them to learn to do this more comfortably. Members tend to hear, accept, and give feedback as they feel less defensive and more open to others in the group. Once they discover what happens as they feel freer and closer to others, they are more apt to share without any planned structure. Members no longer have fears of group exclusion, no longer are afraid of group criticism. On the other hand, the facilitator's role may be questioned, or concerns may emerge about where the group is really going. Low morale may be felt at times. Some group members may attempt to take leadership of the group. As a facilitator, you may feel despair and helplessness unless you know that this is a normal period in a long-term group and a sign of growth. Eventually the group will be ready to look at what is happening. Most importantly, there will be more shared leadership and participation.

Exercises helpful at this stage include:

- 28 Relationships with Women
- 29 Dealing with Conflict
- 30 Personal Power
- 33 Strength Bombardment

Stage 4: Taking Risks and New Behavior

There is less need for structure at this stage. Group members are more likely to take risks and try out new behavior. This can take diverse forms, such as showing caring for another woman, sharing discomforts and reservations, being assertive in the group, and expressing anger. Feelings about self are more positive as individuals behave more independently in and outside the group.

Exercises you can include are:

- 31 Issues in a Group
- 32 Non-Verbal Feedback
- 47 Expressing Anger (see the **Assertiveness Training** section)

Stage 5: Closure and Reentry

It is important to spend one session on closing the group. You can start this process by sharing affection you feel with each other, then move to the grief of leaving, and finally to the joy of going away with new skills and positive feelings about self.

Suggested exercises:

- 33 Strength Bombardment
- 34 Gift Sharing

  ☞ *If you own* **Working With Women's Groups, Volume 2,** *you may also wish to use Exercise 51,* **Appreciation & Regrets,** *from the* **Leadership Skills** *section of that book.*

Don't expect each group to work out as described above; it seldom works that smoothly. Each group varies, as do your feelings about different groups and how each is developing. It is also important to remember that even if one exercise or a group session "bombs," whatever happens contains potential learning for you and the group members if you reflect on the experience.

19 NAMES AND EXPECTATIONS

The group uses this exercise to share their expectations and concerns as well as to develop guidelines for how they want to work together.

GOALS

To include everyone in the group.

To give participants an opportunity to share their hopes and concerns.

To develop group guidelines for working together.

TIME

45 minutes

GROUP SIZE

No more than 30 participants.

MATERIALS

Easel pad and easel; magic markers; masking tape.

PROCESS

Activity 1: Inclusion

1. Start with the following directions:

   ➤ Let's begin this group by learning each other's names and sharing what each of our hopes and concerns are for this group, as well as something interesting about ourselves. Would each person share her name and answer the following open-ended sentences:

   ● My name is . . .

   ● A hope I have is . . . and a concern I have is . . .

   ● One thing that is interesting or unique about me is . . .

2. Begin the activity and continue until all have shared. One of the facilitators may want to record each person's expectations on the easel.

3. Facilitators make appropriate remarks about participants' hopes and concerns.

Activity 2: Expectations and Accountability

1. Note that different and similar expectations have been shared in the group. Tell participants that they are now going to explore these expectations further and examine how they can ensure they will be met.

   ☞ *If there are any expectations that cannot be met in the group, discuss them now.*

2. Instruct participants to find a person who has expectations similar to their own and sit down with that person. Tell them to discuss how each can help the other meet her expectations and how the group might help this happen.

3. After about seven minutes, ask for some sample ideas, especially about how the group could effectively work together and record these under "Group Guidelines/Norms" on an easel.

4. Now ask participants to look around the room and join someone whose expectations are different from their own. Give the pairs the task of discussing how they can help each other meet their dissimilar expectations and how the group can effectively work together.

5. Reconvene the large group and invite participants to share the ideas they had about how they could work effectively around different expectations. Record these on the "Guidelines" list.

6. Continue exploring how participants want to work together as a group, until all the guidelines have been discussed, recorded, and agreed upon by every member of the group. Also ask each group member to be accountable for making sure they and the group follow these guidelines.

20 HOW I SEE MYSELF

In this unique exercise, participants get a chance to interact with others in the group by moving about the room, responding to open ended sentences about themselves.

GOALS

To identify how participants feel about certain areas of their lives.

To practice the skill of self-disclosure.

To begin to get acquainted with the other women in the group.

To discover feelings about women who have chosen a different life style.

TIME

2 hours

GROUP SIZE

Large group of any number and small groups of eight participants.

MATERIALS

Easel paper prepared with open-ended sentences and responses; magic markers; masking tape; pencils and paper.

PROCESS

Activity 1: Lead Sentences

1. Present the goals of the exercise and give the following directions:
   ➤ In a minute we will reveal a lead sentence hanging on the wall. You will find various words or phrases which can be used to complete it on the walls around the room.
   ➤ Be as honest with yourself as possible and choose the word or phrase with which you most closely identify. There may be other words which you feel would fit you better, but select the one from those on the walls which fits you the best.
   ➤ Even if there are two, choose **one** and sit under it.

©1994 Whole Person Press 210 W Michigan Duluth MN 55802   (800) 247-6789

2. Read the first open-ended sentence to the group and the possible responses they can choose from, revealing them to the group as you do. (See **Open-ended Sentences and Responses** on page 84.)

3. Have the participants go to the sign that best fits them.

4. When everyone has chosen a sign to sit under give them the following instructions:

   ➤ Now talk to the others in your subgroup about why each of you selected that particular word or phrase. You will have ten minutes for this discussion.

5. After ten minutes, ask them to take some time to discuss their assumptions about the women sitting under the other words, especially talking about what their assumptions reveal about them personally. Give them about five minutes for this discussion.

   ☞ *Your suggested role in this exercise is to go from group to group to see how each is going and to help any group that might need it. This also gives you some idea of how much time they really need.*

6. After about five minutes, ask for some sample responses to *Step 4* and *Step 5* above.

7. Repeat the process above for another open-ended lead sentence you choose to use. Three or four different sentences is probably enough.

Activity 2: Our Lives

1. Divide the large group into random groups of eight (assigning one facilitator to each group) and move to separate meeting spaces.

2. Lead a discussion about what issues the activity raised about their own life. Some questions to use include:

   ✔ What issues did the activity raise for you?

   ✔ How do you view and feel about yourself at this time?

   ✔ What did the activity help you to discover about your feelings and reactions to women different from yourself?

3. Reconvene the entire group and ask participants to share significant points covered in their small group discussions.

Open-ended Sentences and Responses

Directions to facilitators: Choose the sentences you wish to use from those listed below or develop some that are appropriate to the group. You will not have time to use them all. Put each open-ended sentence and each possible answer on a separate piece of easel paper. As you finish one lead sentence on the easel, take it down and go on to the next (which you placed beneath the first). Use the same process for the completion words and phrases taped on the walls around the room.

One of the primary ways I identify myself is as a . . .

(feminist, mother, wife/life partner, lady, career person)

In regard to my overall appearance I feel . . .

(satisfied and confident, dissatisfied and would like to change how I look, unconcerned, neutral)

My primary goal at this time is to . . .

(develop a close relationship with my partner, have success for my children, lose weight, have sexual fulfillment, achieve success in my career, be successful in school, be a successful homemaker, find a good job, find a life partner)

When I meet a man, the first thing I notice is . . .

(his intelligence, his personality/sex appeal, his physical appearance, how he relates to me, sexist/non-sexist attitudes and behavior, his career/ job)

Generally I feel I am . . .

(insecure and unsure, self-assured and confident, uptight, passive, aggressive)

When it comes to other women, I . . .

(feel close and supportive, feel distant and nontrusting, am looking for friendship and support, would rather be with a man, feel competitive)

It is most important for women to . . .

(be financially independent and support themselves, have a relationship with a man, be beautiful and youthful, have a fulfilling career, be spiritual, have high self-esteem)

21 WHO AM I?

In this two-part exercise, each woman describes parts of herself and then examines how much time she spends on these various aspects, noting any priority discrepancies.

GOALS

To examine how each woman sees herself.

To explore the relationship between how participants view themselves with how they actually spend their time.

TIME

2 hours

GROUP SIZE

Small groups of 8–10 participants; subgroups of 4–5 participants.

MATERIALS

Easel and easel pad; magic markers; masking tape; pencils; note cards (10 cards for each participant); **Time Priorities** worksheet.

PROCESS

Activity 1: Self-Description

1. State the goals of the exercise and distribute cards and pencils.

2. Ask each person to think about how she would describe herself. The descriptions can include roles, personality descriptions, and physical characteristics. Have each participant write down a word or phrase on each note card that describes a part of her.

3. When most are done, ask them to rearrange the cards in order of priority, with the most important aspect of their self-identity placed at the top.

4. Divide the large group into small groups of eight to ten women with a facilitator in each group. Move each group to a separate space.

5. In the small groups, ask each woman to read her descriptions of herself in order of importance. Discourage discussions at this point; the

purpose is to have each woman present to the others without input or judgments how she sees herself.

6. Reconvene the large group and allow time to share insights gained from the activity.

Activity 2: Priority Time

1. Remain in the large group, distribute the worksheet, and read the following directions:

   ➤ Divide the circle into sections like a pie chart according to the amount of time you spend being the different parts of yourself or roles you play in a typical week.

   ➤ Place a "C" by the aspects you have freely chosen for yourself.

      ☞ *Show a sample you have prepared on the easel ahead of time.*

2. Have participants return to their small groups and take turns showing their circle to the group and discussing what they have learned while looking at the amount of time they spend on different facets of themselves. Encourage exploration of any discrepancies between their self-descriptions and amount of time they spend on that part of themselves. Also discuss which parts or roles they have freely chosen and which were imposed on them.

3. After each participant has revealed what she has learned, ask others in the group to state what impact each person's sharing had on them.

Activity 3: Action Planning

1. Divide each small group in half and give the following assignment:

   ➤ Discuss each person's life, helping her look at any changes she would like to make to become more who she wants to be.

   ➤ You have twenty-five minutes to complete this activity, so be sure to divide your time equally.

2. Have the facilitators of the small groups move between the two sub-groups, providing support and help in this process.

3. After about twenty-five minutes, reconvene the large group and close by having each person state:

   ● What she is going to work on and/or something she learned.

   ● How she is feeling about the session.

©1994 Whole Person Press 210 W Michigan Duluth MN 55802   (800) 247-6789

TIME PRIORITIES

Directions: Divide the circle into sections like a pie chart according to the amount of time you spend being the different parts of yourself or roles you play in a typical week. Place a "C" by the aspects you have freely chosen for yourself.

22 LIES ABOUT MYSELF

By lying about their lives, participants are encouraged to assess aspects of themselves they would like to develop as well as new things they would like to include in their lives.

GOALS

To give the participants an opportunity to affirm parts of themselves they have not acknowledged before.

To learn more about who the participants would like to become.

TIME

1 $^1/_2$ hours

GROUP SIZE

Large group of any number and small groups of 6.

MATERIALS

Paper and pencils.

PROCESS

Activity 1: Lies

1. Announce to the group:
   - We are going to look at ourselves by sharing lies about our past and present lives.
   - In examining these lies, we may discover some new aspects of ourselves we did not know before.

2. Ask the participants to find another person to be their partner and sit down with that person.

3. When all the partnerships have been formed, give them the following instructions:
   ➤ Tell each other lies about your past and/or your present life. Each of you will have about five minutes to tell your lies. I will let you know when to switch.

4. After you feel participants have wound down, instruct them to switch and let the other partner lie about her past and/or present.

5. After about five minutes, ask the pairs to discuss their lies, especially sharing how they each felt about who they were in the lies.

6. Distribute paper and pencils to each participant and ask them to list characteristics of themselves that were most prominent in their lies.

7. Join together three pairs to form small groups of six. Instruct them to describe the characteristics of themselves in their lies, emphasizing that they are not to re-tell the lie.

☞ *Participants have a tendency to want to re-tell their whole story.*

8. Have each group discuss the following questions:

☞ *Prepare an easel with the questions in advance or have a facilitator lead each group.*

✔ How do you feel about the characteristics you gave yourself?

✔ Are there any similarities between who you really were (or are) and the characteristics? If yes, describe them.

✔ Do your lies tell anything about your current wishes, how you would like to be or what you would like to do with your life?

✔ How might you change your life to be more like the person in your lie?

✔ Are there common characteristics mentioned by a number of the group members? If so, what does this say to you about our socialization as women?

Closure

1. Reconvene the large group and invite participants to talk about this experience—their feelings and what they learned—and what it affirmed about themselves.

2. Close by encouraging them to develop more of the parts of themselves that they would like to be.

VARIATION

■ Try conducting this activity twice: the first time use lies about the past, the second use lies about the present.

■ As an icebreaker, ask each participant to share three things about herself, including one that is not true. Have the group try to guess which is the lie.

23 LIFE GOALS

Using a handout, participants determine what specific goals they have for their lives and explore ways to achieve them.

GOALS

To determine the goals each woman has for her life.

To identify which goals are priorities.

To examine ways each woman is or is not accomplishing her goals.

To set some action plans to better accomplish goals that are priorities.

TIME

1 ½ hours

GROUP SIZE

Any number of small groups of 6.

MATERIALS

Easel and easel paper; magic markers; masking tape; pencils; **Possible Goals For My Life** worksheet.

PROCESS

Activity 1: Goals

1. Distribute the worksheet and pencils and give the following introduction:
   - Everyone—perhaps even without realizing it—has set goals they hope to meet during their lifetime.
   - However, not all of us are clear about what those goals are.
   - Today we are going to determine what specific goals we have set for ourselves.

2. Read the instructions for filling out the handout:
   - ➤ Read all of the goals on the page, then pick the five you would most like to achieve.

➤ Next, rank the five goals from one to five, with one as "my most important priority." You will have ten minutes for these tasks.

3. After ten minutes, call time and divide participants into small groups of six.

4. Have each woman share her top five goals in order of priority. Then ask her the following questions in order to explore these areas:

☞ *The other group members are invited to give supportive input.*

✔ How are you working to achieve these goals right now?

✔ Are there any goals you want, but feel you are not spending enough time on? If so, which ones?

✔ If you were able to look through the eyes of your future self, how would the world look different?

✔ What more do you need to do to achieve your goals? What are some specific actions you could take right now that would help you get closer to your goals?

Closure

1. Reconvene the large group and invite participants to share what they have learned about life goals and achievement of those goals.

2. Encourage them to continue working on achieving their priority goals.

©1994 Whole Person Press 210 W Michigan Duluth MN 55802   (800) 247-6789

POSSIBLE GOALS FOR MY LIFE

Directions: The following are some goals you may have for your life at this point. Read all of them and then choose the top five for yourself. (There is space to add any goals that are not on this list.) Then go back and rank the five goals from one to five, with one as the most important and five as the least important.

❏ A successful, fulfilling career (paid or volunteer)

❏ Accomplishment in education (high school, college degree, PhD, etc.)

❏ Emotional stability—peace of mind

❏ Close, supportive relationships with other women

❏ Sexual fulfillment

❏ Community/world involvement (working on projects to help my community/world become a better and more humane place)

❏ Having and nurturing children

❏ Material possessions (house, car, vacations, clothes)

❏ Healthy body

❏ Intimate, close, fulfilling relationship with a life partner

❏ Self-acceptance and high self-esteem

❏ Own a business or be successful in my business

❏ Free time

❏ Develop a skill or interest I have (name it)

❏ Become a community leader and/or run for public office

❏ Lose weight

❏ Others?

24 DREAMS AND POSSIBILITIES

Through a variety of activities, participants explore their dreams and develop ways of bringing them to life.

GOALS

To give an opportunity for women to explore their dreams.

To provide a way to connect their dreams with possible objectives in order to begin to achieve them.

TIME

3 $\frac{1}{2}$ hours

GROUP SIZE

Small groups of 6–8 participants.

MATERIALS

Easel and easel pad; magic markers; masking tape; paper and pencils; **In My Life** worksheet; **My Action Plan** worksheet.

PROCESS

Activity 1: Ice Breaker

1. Use the following as an introduction:
   - Today we are going to take time to dream about ourselves.
   - We will then connect these dreams with specific objectives so we can begin to achieve them.
2. Divide the participants into small groups of six to eight.
3. In each small group, give the following instructions:
   ➤ Choose something from your purse or pocket that is significant about your life or symbolizes what is important to your life.
4. Give them a few minutes to choose their object and then have each person show hers to the group and discuss its importance to her life.

Activity 2: Fantasy

1. To start them in a fantasy process, ask this question of the group

   ✔ If you could do anything for a year, with no obstacles in your way, what would you do?

2. Go around the group until each person answes the question above.

3. Distribute the **In My Life** worksheet and tell them:

   ➤ Continue to dream. This time list fifteen fantasies of what you would like to be doing two to five years from now.

   > ☞ *Often women find it difficult to think of this many items, but encourage them to try, no matter how far out the fantasy seems. In fact, it will help to ask them to really fantasize; e.g., not just "I want to become a manager in the crafts store," but "I want to own my own crafts store."*

4. After they have completed *Step 3*, instruct members to check their top three fantasies.

5. Then ask each person to share their fantasies with the group. Have them save their paper for later use.

Activity 2: Successes and Accomplishments

1. Divide the small groups in two and move each group to a separate place.

2. Explain the task:

   ➤ We want to explore our successes in life, things that we have done well and feel good about. Each of you will have time to share your successes in this subgroup.

   ➤ The others will serve as coaches and one as a recorder. The coaches will probe for the skills involved with your successes or accomplishments. The recorder's role is to record the successes and list the skills involved on the easel paper.

   ➤ Distribute your time equally, about fifteen minutes per person.

3. After forty-five minutes or when the subgroups are finished, distribute a blank sheet of paper to each participant and describe the next task to the subgroups:

   ➤ Write a brief autobiography that might appear in **Who's Who Among American Women.** It doesn't have to be a typical list of accomplishments traditionally recognized in such collections.

➤ Do not write an obituary. Write what you would like to have said about you and what you might be able to accomplish.

➤ When you have finished, you will have a chance to take turns reading your autobiography to each other.

4. After about twelve minutes, ask them to read their autobiographies to each other in their subgroups.

Turning Dreams into Reality

1. Ask participants to find their **In My Life** worksheet and review their top three fantasies to determine if they are still their top choices or if they want to add or change something.

2. Ask them to choose the one dream from the top three they would most like to achieve in the next five years.

3. Distribute the **My Action Plan** worksheet and tell them to return to their small subgroups.

4. Give the following directions:

➤ Share your dream and discuss what you could do right now to begin to make the dream a reality.

➤ Help each other identify specific objectives, keeping in mind the skills you identified in the previous activity.

➤ Try to come up with specific tasks for yourself and a timetable for accomplishing them. You have thirty minutes for this task.

Closure

1. Reconvene the large group.

2. Give time for each woman to present her contract with herself: what she is going to do to fulfill one of her dreams.

3. When all have shared, encourage them to support each other in the accomplishment of these dreams by talking to each other periodically to see how each one is doing in accomplishing these dreams.

IN MY LIFE

Instructions: List your fantasies of what you would like to be doing two to five years from now.

1.

2.

3.

4.

5.

6.

7.

8.

9.

10.

11.

12.

13.

14.

15.

MY ACTION PLAN FOR ACCOMPLISHING MY DREAM

My Dream _____

_____

_____

Specific Objectives (To accomplish my dream):

1.

2.

3.

4.

Tasks	**By When**
1.	
2.	
3.	
4.	
5.	
6.	

©1994 Whole Person Press 210 W Michigan Duluth MN 55802   (800) 247-6789

25 BODY AWARENESS

Using body exploration and drawing "self-portraits," participants are encouraged to examine how their self-esteem and body image are closely linked.

GOALS

To help women become more aware of how they feel about their bodies.

To have women share with each other their feelings and perceptions of their own bodies.

To examine how a woman's self-esteem and self-confidence is often closely linked to her own body image.

TIME

2 ¹/₂ hours

GROUP SIZE

Any number in the large group; small groups of 8.

MATERIALS

Easel chart paper; multi-colored magic markers; masking tape.

PROCESS

Activity 1: Body Exploration

1. Introduce the exercise with the following chalktalk:
   - Today we will start by focusing on becoming more aware of how each of us views our own bodies.
   - Later we will share our feelings and perceptions with one another.

2. Tell the participants you are going to start with a body exploration activity. Ask them to find a comfortable place in the room, apart from others with enough room so they can lie down. Encourage them to remove extra clothing like sweaters and shoes so they can be as comfortable as possible.

☞ *The facilitator giving the instructions below should also par-*
ticipate in the body exploration activity, otherwise group mem-
bers may feel they are being watched. Inform the groups of the
facilitators' participation before you begin. Do not move too
quickly through this exploration. Take your time with each part.

3. When everyone has a space and is lying down, read the **Body Exploration** reading on page 101.

4. When most are sitting up, ask them to form groups of eight with a
facilitator to discuss the experience, using questions such as:

✔ What happened for you during the exploration activity? When were
you comfortable? Uncomfortable?

✔ How did you feel touching your body? Were there parts of your body
you found difficult to touch, or off limits? Which ones?

✔ What did you discover your feelings were toward your body during
that activity?

☞ *Women usually have a variety of responses to this activity.*
Some may choose not to do the activity or only parts of it.
What is important is to encourage and accept the verbaliza-
tion of any of their feelings.

Activity 2: Body Image

1. Tell the group that they are going to have an opportunity to explore how
they view their body in a more graphic way. Distribute an easel sheet
to each person and markers.

2. Ask each woman to draw a picture of how she views her body.
Encourage them to be creative and not worry about their drawing
skill—the picture is to represent visually or symbolically how they
view and feel about their body.

3. When most are finished, ask the women to move into their small groups
to share and discuss their pictures.

4. Give each woman an opportunity to show and talk about her "body
picture" with the small group and to get their reactions to it (especially
the impact the drawing had on them). As a facilitator you can help each
one explore particular areas by asking:

✔ Are there parts of your body you especially like? Which ones?

✔ Are there parts of your body you do not like or wish were different? Is this something you can and want to change? Or do you want to accept this part and begin to love it?

✔ Are there parts of your body that you have already changed, either surgically or through your own efforts? How do you feel about these efforts now?

✔ Overall, how do you feel about your body? How do you show this?

> ☞ *A woman's body-self portrait is often very revealing, both to herself and others. Talking about our body images usually leads to intensive and worthwhile sharing. However, a few women may be reluctant to show their pictures to the group. Encourage them, but do not push too hard. This is a very difficult area for some to examine; they may not be ready to do so.*

5. After each participant has shared and talked about her picture, begin a discussion by asking the group the following question:

✔ What is the relationship between our body image and our level of self-confidence or self-esteem?

Closure

1. Reconvene the large group and make some appropriate closing remarks about the work everyone has done.

2. Invite comments about the session, especially what participants have learned or want to work on.

VARIATION

■ If you feel uncomfortable with Activity 1, you could eliminate it and move directly into Activity 2.

Body Exploration Reading

Today we're going to explore how we feel about out bodies. We will start by gently caring for our bodies.

Relax your body and gently close your eyes.

Get in touch with your breathing . . . Is it deep or shallow . . . rapid or slow?

Find the tension areas of your body . . . Tell each tense part to relax . . . Feel your body sink into the floor . . . into your space. . . .

Now with your fingertips begin to explore your hands . . . Are they cold or warm . . . soft or rough?

Move up your arms to your shoulders. Are your shoulders pointed . . . or round . . . tense or relaxed?

Explore all sides of your neck . . . Is it tensed or relaxed?

Move to your face . . . your eyes . . . your nose . . . Is it long or short? . . . your cheeks . . . your mouth . . . your ears . . . Feel your hair . . . Is it coarse or soft . . . curly or straight . . . long or short?

Move your hands to your chest . . . exploring your breasts . . . Are they flat or round . . . small or large . . . Are either of your breasts missing or reconstructed?

Go down to your waist . . . Is it thick or thin? . . . to your hips . . . your buttocks . . . Over to your stomach . . . is it soft or hard?

Explore your genital area . . . your thighs and legs . . . are they hairy or smooth?

Feel your feet . . . including each toe.

Now gently bring your hands back to rest . . . This is your own body . . . uniquely yours . . . a special body.

When you feel ready open your eyes and sit up.

26 ROMANCE: AN ADDICTION

By examining their ideals about romance and love and assessing previous relationships, participants develop a better understanding of the role romance has played in their relationships.

GOALS

To better understand what part romance plays in women's ideas about relationships.

To identify each person's relationship patterns.

To explore the connection between self-esteem and intimacy.

TIME

2 $\frac{1}{2}$ hours

GROUP SIZE

Any number of small groups of 8–10.

MATERIALS

Easels and easel pad; magic markers; masking tape; pencils; **Relationship Patterns** worksheet.

PROCESS

Activity 1: Ice Breaker

1. Ask each person to answer the following open ended sentences:
   ✔ Romance is . . .
   ✔ Love is . . .
   ✔ When I fall in love I . . .
   ✔ When someone falls in love with me I . . .

2. Discuss their answers, identifying any commonalities.

Activity 2: Romantic Myths

1. In small groups, have participants identify and explore the myths about love and romance found in novels, soap operas, and movies. Record these on an easel.

2. Discuss the major themes about romance that we as women learn.

Activity 3: Relationship Patterns

1. Tell participants they are going to have an opportunity to explore patterns that occur in their close relationships.

2. Distribute the worksheet and ask them to take some time to answer the questions. Give them fifteen or twenty minutes.

3. Have participants share their responses and what they learned through this self-reflection. Some questions you may want to ask are:

   ✔ Do you note any patterns in your relationships? If so, what are they?

   ✔ Are you waiting to make basic decisions in your life until you have a significant relationship with a future partner, e.g., postponing buying a house until Mr. or Ms. Right comes along?

   ✔ Is there a difference in how you feel about yourself if you are alone or with someone?

     ☞ *Some women find themselves overeating, overdrinking, or getting depressed when they are not involved with someone.*

   ✔ Is your focus in life on developing and growing yourself or on trying to change others? What might this mean for you?

   ✔ Do you need to "be in love" or have someone "in love with you"? What impact does being in love have on you and what happens when you or the other person falls out of love?

Activity 4: Relationship Changes

1. Form groups of four and have participants share with each other the changes they would like to make in their present ideas about romance and relationships.

2. Invite participants to share their responses with the total group.

3. End with a chalktalk based on the following statements:

   ● Low self-esteem is a major barrier to intimate relationships. If we are trying to change our partners we are not focused on our own life.

● The more we try to meet the "right" person, the less we develop ourselves and the less chance we will become whole, complete persons.

● The more we develop ourselves, the greater chance we will meet someone who is also a growing and together person.

VARIATIONS

■ As part of (or instead of) Activity 1, ask participants to stand if they read romance novels and then ask those standing to share why they read them.

■ Contact participants prior to this exercise and assign individuals to read novels, stories, or magazine articles and analyze their romantic themes. You could also use movies and television programs. This works particularly well as a task for a women's studies course.

©1994 Whole Person Press 210 W Michigan Duluth MN 55802 (800) 247-6789

RELATIONSHIP PATTERNS

Directions: Choose three of your most significant intimate relationships in the last five to ten years and answer the questions below for each of the relationships. Then look at your answers and see if there are any patterns.

Questions	Names of partners in past relationships			Patterns (?)
1. How were you feeling about yourself when the relationship began?				
2. How did you react when it ended?				
3. How long did the relationship last?				
4. How much "in love" were you?				
5. Did the relationship cause your self-esteem to remain the same, go down, or go up?				
6. Did you feel you had to wear a "mask" in the relationship? What was the "mask"?				
7. Was jealousy a major part of it?				
8. What was the power equation?				
9. What did the other person have that you wanted/longed for in yourself?				
10. Did you try to change him/her? How?				

27 SEXUAL EXPERIENCES

In this intense exercise, participants share their sexual experiences, responding to a number of ideas and questions and then identifying sexual patterns they may want to change.

GOALS

To give an opportunity for women to share and explore their sexual experiences.

To better understand personal sexual attitudes and behaviors and how they are connected to the past.

To identify sexual patterns participants wish to change.

TIME

3 hours

GROUP SIZE

Any number of small groups of 9–10 participants.

MATERIALS

A bell or some other attention-getting device.

PROCESS

Introduction

1. Introduce the exercise with the following statement:
   - This session will give us the opportunity to better understand our sexual attitudes and behaviors and how they are connected to our past experiences.
2. Ask the members to find two other persons with whom they would like to spend at least an hour sharing past sexual experiences and feelings.

   ☞ *It is important for them to choose women with whom they feel support and comfort.*

3. Tell each trio to find a comfortable place, apart from the others, but within hearing distance of the facilitator.

Activity 1: Sharing Experiences

☞ This activity may raise some traumatic or intense experiences participants have repressed or not discussed with others, such as rape or sexual abuse. Skilled facilitators should be available during the activity in case any participants need special support. Also allow enough time for discussion after the activity.

1. Explain the following procedure:

   ➤ I will be giving you a number of questions to discuss.

   ➤ Each of you will have a few minutes to share your experiences, if you wish—it's O.K. not to talk. If you can't recall any experiences, you may find that someone else's may stimulate a memory.

   ➤ Try not to spend too much time with one person as I will be moving you on to another set of questions every eight to twelve minutes.

   ➤ Discuss only the questions given you; more questions will follow.

   ☞ Don't give all the topics/questions ahead of time. Participants should have equal time for each area and be encouraged to move along. Choose the questions you want to include from the list on pages 109 and 110. Read each question. Continue giving the questions every eight to twelve minutes. If you have a large group, it is helpful to have a bell or some way to get the trios' attention, other than by voice when you are ready to move to the next set of questions.

Closure

1. Join three trios together with a facilitator(s) to discuss the experience.

2. Allow time for ventilation about the activity using these questions:

   ✔ How are you feeling?

   ✔ What feelings or awarenesses did the activity bring up for you?

   ☞ If someone shares a traumatic experience—that she was abused or raped—make sure she receives appropriate support and response from the other women. Make certain to follow-up with her individually to suggest counseling or to help her contact a crisis support center.

3. Some additional questions to help process the activity include:

   ✔ Did you find any common experiences/feelings with the other women in your trio? If so what were they?

✔ What are some connections between your past and present sexual feelings, thoughts, and behavior patterns?

✔ Are there any current sexual patterns in your life you would like to change? Which ones? Why?

4. Reconvene the entire group and ask participants for their reactions to the session.

5. Make appropriate comments to close the session.

VARIATION

■ If you are working with an on-going support group of less than ten women, consider having participants answer every question in the large group (without dividing into trios). Select those questions that are most relevant to your group.

©1994 Whole Person Press 210 W Michigan Duluth MN 55802   (800) 247-6789

Questions about our sexual experiences

1. How did your parents express affection toward each other, yourself, and other family members? How did you feel about this? How did your family "handle" nudity and how did they talk about sex;e.g., what words were used to describe body parts?

2. Recall how you first became aware of your parent's or other adult's sexuality. How did you feel about what you saw, heard? Did they explain anything about this to you? If so, what did they say and what feelings did they convey?

3. What early memories do you have of masturbation as an infant or child? What did your parents or other adults say or do about it? What memories do you have of sex play with other children? What were your feelings about this? If your parents/other adults knew, how did they react?

4. What and how did you learn about sex from other girls as you were growing up. What and how did you learn from boys? How did you respond and feel about that information or those experiences?

5. What memories do you have of touching and sex exploration with other girls in late childhood and early adolescence? What were your feelings about these experiences?

6. How did you find out about menstruation? What message did you receive? When did you get your first period? What did you do and feel when it happened? What are your feelings about menstruation now? What words do you use to describe it?

7. What were your feelings about breast development (or lack of it)? Do you recall the first time you wore a bra? What led up to wanting one and getting it? Did you ever wear a padded bra? If so, what did you hope would happen by wearing it? What were your fears? Were you ever called any names because of your breast size?

8. In adolescence what behavior and attributes determined whether or not you were feminine? How did you measure up to the social criteria of femininity? Did you give up/change any of your behavior or favorite activities at this time? Was there a change in your relationships with others of the same and opposite sex at this time? Were you aware of any sexual feelings during this period and how did you handle these?

9. What were your relationships with members of the other sex in

©1994 Whole Person Press 210 W Michigan Duluth MN 55802   (800) 247-6789

adolescence? Do you recall the first time you went out with a boy? What happened? How did you feel? What are your memories of the first time you were kissed or touched sexually by a boy? What was this first sexual experience like and how did you feel about it?

10. Some women have had relationships only with women in their lives. If this is true for you or if you had sexual relationships with women, what are your memories of the first time you were kissed or touched sexually by a girl or woman? What was this first sexual experience like and how did you feel about it?

11. What are your memories about the first time a sexual relationship ended? Who initiated it and how did you react?

12. What does the word virgin mean to you? How did you feel about being one? When and how did you make a decision to have sexual intercourse, if you have? Or was it forced on you? What was this first experience like? How do you feel about sexual intercourse now?

13. What memories do you have of the first time you ever experienced an orgasm? How did it happen and how did you feel? If you have not had an orgasm yet, what are your experiences of and feelings about trying to have one (if you have tried)? Have you ever pretended to have an orgasm? What were your reasons for faking it?

14. Have your sexual relationships been mostly satisfying (emotionally and physically) or unsatisfying? Who usually initiates sex or a sexual advance and how do you feel about this? How do you communicate to your partner what you want and like sexually?

15. Have you ever had a sexual encounter such as date rape or sexual abuse when you did not feel like it? What contributed to your going against your own feelings? If sex has ever been forced upon you, how did it happen and how did you react and feel at the time?

16. What was your worst sexual experience? What about this experience made it bad for you?

17. What sexual moments or sexual relationships have felt best to you or been the most pleasurable?

18. What are your feelings about the last hour? How do you feel towards each other?

©1994 Whole Person Press 210 W Michigan Duluth MN 55802   (800) 247-6789

28 RELATIONSHIPS WITH WOMEN

In this active exercise, participants form pairs to examine supportive and nonsupportive relationships. Feedback is encouraged.

GOALS

To become aware of the different feelings women have about each other.

To encourage feedback to each woman about how she is perceived by other women.

To examine how women in support relationships behave toward one another.

TIME

1 ¹/₂ hours

GROUP SIZE

Any number of participants, usually the members of an on-going group.

MATERIALS

None.

PROCESS

Activity 1: Pairing

1. Present the goals and rationale for this session.

2. Ask the group members to stand up and walk around the room making no contact with others, getting in touch with how that feels to them.

3. After about a minute give them the following instructions:

   ➤ Now begin to make eye contact with others as you continue to walk around. Try to be aware of how this feels.

   ➤ Now as you continue walking, be aware of who you feel support from in this room.

   ➤ When you feel ready, go to one of the support persons, if she is willing to be with you, and express the supportive feeling with that person nonverbally.

©1994 Whole Person Press 210 W Michigan Duluth MN 55802   (800) 247-6789

➤ Then sit down and share what support means for you.

4. After five minutes, invite the pairs to share with the whole group what contributed to them feeling support from the woman they paired with.

5. Ask everyone to stand up again. This time have them choose a person they have not felt support from (or feel uncomfortable with) and express this feeling nonverbally with that person. Then ask them to sit down and discuss what the nonsupport or discomfort is about.

6. After about five minutes, encourage the pairs to share with the large group what kinds of attitudes and behaviors contributed to them not feeling support from their partner and if that had changed any during their discussion.

7. Continue the above process, this time having them choose a person with whom they feel support or comfort. However, in the verbal aspect, ask them to take a risk in what they share with the person.

  ☞ *The rationale behind this activity is that usually we hold back risky things that might, we feel, have a negative affect on a relationship that is comfortable, trying to keep it safe. However, to continue to build intimacy and trust in relationships, it is important to share negative as well as positive feelings.*

8. Ask participants what has happened when they took a risk.

Activity 2: Unfinished Business

1. There may be some relationship issues that have not been explored or worked through during the above activity. You may want to give time in the group to work further on individual relationships and explore any unresolved feelings. Do this work in the large group.

2. When you have finished this work move on to closing the session by sharing what each participant has learned.

Closure

1. In the large group, ask participants to verbalize what they have learned, the feelings they have about their relationships with women, and how they can be more supportive of and more open to support from women.

2. Have participants identify how women in supportive relationships behave toward one another.

VARIATION

■ You may wish to use other pairings for Activity 1, such as, "Choose someone you . . .

- ● . . . would like to play with."
- ● . . . have unresolved feelings toward."
- ● . . . are curious about."
- ● . . . would like to work with."
- ● . . . feel affection toward."

©1994 Whole Person Press 210 W Michigan Duluth MN 55802   (800) 247-6789

29 DEALING WITH CONFLICT

This engaging exercise helps participants identify ways they typically respond to conflict and how they as women have been taught to respond to conflict.

GOALS

To give an opportunity for participants to discover how they handle conflict.

To increase their awareness of their feelings in conflict situations.

To identify ways women have been taught to respond to conflict.

TIME

2 hours

GROUP SIZE

Any number of small groups of 6 or 8.

MATERIALS

Easel and easel paper; magic markers; masking tape; pencils or pens; a money container; **Conflict Reflection Questions** worksheet.

PROCESS

Activity 1: Money

1. Without discussing the goals, ask individuals to give a reasonable sum of money (fifty cents to two dollars) to one of the facilitators.

   ☞ *Determine the exact amount after participants are divided into small groups by asking them to decide together on an amount they can afford and yet is high enough to ensure they have an investment in the activity.*

   Do not say why you want the money, other than that it will be used in the next activity. Ask them to trust you.

2. Divide the group into groups of six or eight participants, without a facilitator. Have them sit in separate spaces in the group room.

3. Give the following directions:

➤ Your task is to decide who in your small group will get the money.

    ☞ *Tell each group the amount the person will receive when a decision is made (divide the money collected evenly between the groups).*

➤ Use the following rules:

    ➣ The decision must be unanimous.

    ➣ Only one person gets the money.

    ➣ The person receiving the money must use the money on herself and not for someone else or for a cause. It can not be redistributed after the activity.

        ☞ *The rationale: It is difficult for many women to directly ask for something for herself, because it goes against women's socialization, which is to be "unselfish." It's more okay if it is for others or a worthwhile cause.*

    ➣ If a decision is not made in twenty minutes, I will either keep the money or send it to an unworthy cause (announce the cause).

4. Explain the facilitators' roles.

    ☞ *A facilitator should be available to observe each group's process, sitting outside each group or moving around the groups if there is not a facilitator for each group.*

5. Set the clock and tell the groups to start.

6. After twenty minutes, call time and give the money to the person the group designated. If the group has not made a decision, the facilitator keeps the money.

7. Give each group ten minutes to ventilate, sharing the reactions they had during the activity and how they are feeling now that it is over.

Activity 2: Conflict

1. Distribute the worksheet and pencils, asking participantsto reflect alone, answering the questions on the worksheet.

2. Have the facilitators join the small groups they observed and ask the participants to use the worksheet questions to help discuss and examine what happened and what they can learn from the experience.

    ☞ *During this discussion the facilitators may also want to share their observations in a nonjudgmental way.*

✔ What did you want in this activity? Did you get it? If you did, how did you get it? If not, what prevented you?

✔ How do you feel about yourself as a result of this activity?

✔ What did you do and feel when conflict emerged in your group? Is this a habitual way you have of dealing with conflict?

✔ What is your level of satisfaction with how you dealt with the conflict?

✔ What would you like to do differently next time conflict occurs?

✔ How do you feel toward the other group members? What contributed to this feeling?

3. Reconvene the large group and have each small group take turns sitting in the center of the room in a circle facing each other. Give them time to share what they learned about dealing with conflict as women as the other groups listen.

4. Close out the session with appropriate remarks.

VARIATION

■ If you want to increase the conflict dynamics of Activity 2, put the money in the center of each group just before they start the activity. However, be prepared for the possibility that a participant may just take the money.

■ If you have time after each group has shared their feelings about conflict, encourage questions—especially concerning process—from the other groups.

CONFLICT REFLECTION QUESTIONS

1. What did you want in this activity?

2. Did you get what you wanted? If you did, how did you get it? If not, what prevented you?

3. How do you feel about yourself as a result of this activity?

4. What did you do and feel when conflict emerged in your group? Is this a habitual way you have of dealing with conflict?

5. What is your level of satisfaction with how you dealt with the conflict?

6. What would you like to do differently next time conflict occurs?

7. How do you feel toward the other group members? What contributed to this feeling?

30 PERSONAL POWER

Using a fun, "power line-up" and feedback from the group, participants explore how they use their power.

GOALS

To examine how each women has used her personal power in the group.

To discover what the issues surrounding power are for women in the group.

To identify how women feel about other women who they perceive have and use power.

TIME

1 $\frac{1}{2}$ – 3 hours (depending on whether you choose to conduct Activity 3)

GROUP SIZE

10–20 participants (best if used with ongoing or weekend groups).

MATERIALS

Easel and easel pad; magic markers; masking tape; note cards; pencils or pens.

PROCESS

Activity 1: Power Line Up

1. Present the goals of the session and segue into the first task by saying:

   ● In order to better explore the power issues in this group, we are going to participate in an activity that will help us start to look at power.

2. Ask the participants to stand up and instruct them to form a line from the most powerful to the least powerful in the group. Tell them to move themselves until they are satisfied with where they are in the line.

   ☞ *At this point do not define power for them if they ask, just tell them to give it their own definition for this activity. There will probably be a lot of movement for a short period of time as the women keep shifting their position in the line. The facilitators should also participate in this activity.*

3. After the women have basically stopped moving in the line, stop the activity and reproduce the order in the line on an easel.

4. Encourage a discussion of their ratings of themselves and their feelings in forming the line. Use the following questions:

✔ How did you feel before, during, and after the activity? If your feelings changed, what contributed to the changes?

✔ What is the definition of power you were using?

   ☞ *You may want to record each person's definition and make sure everyone responds to this question.*

✔ Was there any point during the activity when you wanted to change your position and did? How did you feel about this and what happened? Was there any time when you wanted to but did not change your position? What prevented you from moving?

Activity 2: Pair Discussion

1. Ask them to form pairs with a person who was next to them in the line up.

2. Ask them to share their responses to the following questions, each in turn answering aloud the whole set of questions before the other begins. They are to answer the whole set of questions three times, alternating.

   ☞ *Have the questions prepared ahead of time on an easel sheet and hanging where all can see.*

✔ I use my power when . . .

✔ I overestimate others' power by . . .

✔ I "make" myself feel powerless when I . . .

3. After about ten minutes, give the pairs a warning to finish and then ask them to move back to the group.

4. Reconvene the group and lead a discussion about their answers.

Activity 3: Power Feedback (optional)

   ☞ *This activity works best when you are conducting a group that has worked together for a while, such as an on-going support group. It is not recommended for use with groups whose participants are unfamiliar with one another.*

1. Give the following instructions:

➤ All of us have power and use it in this group and with others.

➤ Think of the impact each person's use of power has had on you. Some have had a positive impact; some had a negative impact.

➤ For each person in the group, write on a note card the type of power they have used, especially one type that was positive and one that has been negative for you.

➤ Be specific, citing an experience if possible. Sign each card.

2. When they have finished, have group members distribute their cards to each other. Give time for each person to read their cards.

3. Then spend time with each person, giving them time to share their feelings about the feedback they received and to ask questions about the feedback. Explore more fully the information they received about their use of power in the group. Questions you may want to ask to help them explore power issues include:

✔ Do most group members have the same perceptions of your power?

✔ Were you surprised by anything?

✔ Do you see yourself as using your power in the same way others see it?

✔ Is there a different impact you would like to make on others? If so, how might you go about it?

✔ Do you use your power in the same way around men? If not, in what ways and why might you be different around men?

Closure

1. In pairs, ask participants to identify one or two ways they would like to increase their use of power in a positive way.

2. End the exercise by inviting each participant to tell the group in what new ways she would like to use power.

VARIATION

■ As an option to end Activity 2, lead a discussion about the times when participants have felt powerful and times when they have felt powerless. You may want to record this information on an easel in order to examine any patterns. DO NOT use this variation if you choose to conduct Activity 3.

31 ISSUES IN A GROUP

This exercise helps to bring any issues in the group to the surface in an innovative and physical way.

GOALS

To provide a means of raising some of the issues in the group.

To have some fun.

TIME

2 hours

GROUP SIZE

On-going small group of 8–10.

MATERIALS

Easel and easel paper; magic markers; masking tape; a foam rubber bat or newspaper rolled into a tube-like bat.

PROCESS

Activity 1: The Bat

☞ *This exercise is helpful when you think there are issues, especially conflict, in an on-going small group, which have not surfaced yet. The "bat" provides a tool for a different kind of interaction.*

1. Throw the "bat" in the middle of the group and explain:

   ● We thought it might be helpful to look at some issues in our group, and have fun doing it.

   ● This thing in the middle of the floor could represent anything. Nonverbally do whatever you wish with it with anyone here.

   ● Let's see what happens. Anyone can begin.

2. Let interaction occur until you feel you have enough data to process, then stop the action (fifteen to twenty minutes should be enough time).

   ☞ *The interactions that often occur in groups include passing the bat to others, beating it on the floor, playing a game with it,*

*juggling it, hitting someone, holding a tug of war, ripping parts
of it up (if paper), giving it to someone with affection, rubbing
someone's back with it, dancing with it, and throwing it out of the
group.*

Activity 2: Issues Reflection

1. To examine what happened, first ask everyone to express what they
   are feeling.

2. Then ask them to identify specific pieces of the interaction they would
   like to discuss or explore (list on an easel).

3. Take the pieces given priority and examine them one at a time by using
   the following questions:

   ✔ What happened?

   ✔ Does everyone recall when that happened?

   ✔ What were your reactions?

   ✔ What were your feelings and thoughts?

   ✔ What were the possible reasons for your reactions in this situation?

   ✔ What issue did this raise?

   ✔ What does this mean?

   ✔ Based on what we have said and heard, what conclusions can we draw?

   ✔ What do we need to say or do to resolve any issues?

   ✔ How could we apply what we have been discussing to other situations?

   ☞ *You might suggest talking about the way the group members
   responded to the bat—was it typical socialized female behavior,
   atypical behavior, or a combination of both?*

4. As closure for this session, ask individuals to say how they felt about the
   group.

32 NONVERBAL FEEDBACK

Best when used with an on-going group, this exercise uses nonverbal feedback to help groups further increase their trust and intimacy.

GOALS

To practice giving and receiving feedback.

To discover feelings about giving and receiving nonverbal communication.

To learn to take risks.

TIME

2 hours

GROUP SIZE

An on-going group of 8–12 participants.

MATERIALS

None

PROCESS

Activity 1: Non-verbal Feedback

🖙 *This activity should be done only after a group has been together for some time and has built some trust and member inclusion. Even at this point, there may be initial resistance to participating in this experience. Give participants time to ventilate their feelings about participating, but not so much time that their feelings are dissipated. If the group agrees to engage in this activity, it is sometimes helpful if one of the facilitators begins to model the variety of ways of giving nonverbal feedback by going first.*

1. State the goals, describe the activity, and check with group members to see if they are willing to participate in this activity.

2. Ask everyone to stand in a circle. Have whoever wants to go first stand in front of the person next to her, determine how she is feeling toward that person, and then express these feelings to her nonverbally. The

person receiving the nonverbal feedback may respond nonverbally if she wishes. Continue this process with the first person giving feedback to everyone in the circle. Then have another person go around the circle and give nonverbal feedback. Only one person is to give feedback at a time.

3. After three or four have given feedback, it is helpful to sit down and process what has happened thus far. Persons receiving feedback may want to ask what someone meant in their nonverbal communication and/or to say how they felt. Persons giving feedback may want to check out how they were perceived and share how they felt while giving the nonverbal feedback.

4. Stand up again and continue the feedback. Continue the procedure above (*Step 2* and *Step 3*) until all who want have given non-verbal feedback.

Activity 2: Feedback Temperature

1. Discuss the following questions in the large group:
   - ✔ What were you most comfortable with—giving or receiving feedback? What are the reasons?
   - ✔ Did you take any risks during the activity? If so, what risks and how do you feel about this?
   - ✔ If you gave nonverbal feedback, were you honest about your feelings or did you hold back? If so, when?
   - ✔ Was there someone you wanted different feedback from than what you received? If yes, how do you feel about this and did you share your feelings with that person? If no, would you be willing now to say something to that person?
   - ✔ Did you learn anything about the ways in which you give and receive feedback, especially about behavior you would like to change?

2. Invite participants to continue the feedback process in the group. Also encourage them to give and request feedback from each other as well as from people in their lives outside the group.

33 STRENGTH BOMBARDMENT

This uplifting closing activity lets each woman listen to and receive written positive feedback from other group members. Perfect when many participants have self-esteem issues.

GOALS

To give and receive positive feedback.

To increase each woman's self-esteem through positive reinforcement.

TIME

1 ¹/₂ hours

GROUP SIZE

An on-going small group of 8–12 participants

MATERIALS

Paper and pencils.

PROCESS

Activity 1: Positive Reinforcement

☞ *This activity is useful when most of the women in the group have a low self-image or could benefit from some positive reinforcement. It is also an excellent activity to use as you are closing the group.*

1. Distribute paper and pencils and describe the task:

    ➤ We are going to experiment with giving and receiving positive feedback in the group.

    ➤ Take five minutes and write down any strengths that you feel you have as a person.

    ➤ Include anything you like about yourself: skills you have, positive personality characteristics, something positive you did in the group or outside the group, etc.

2. After five minutes, ask participants to put their papers aside. One at a time, as they volunteer, a person receives positive feedback from the

rest of the group. Before the group begins, have the recipient ask someone to write down her feedback as it is given.

   ☞ *If this is the closing exercise for the group, the women then have this list to take home with them as a reminder of their positive traits.*

3. After each woman hears her feedback, have the person recording give her the written response. You may want to ask how she's feeling and how her list of strengths compares with what she heard others say.

4. Continue this process until all have received feedback, including the facilitators.

Closure

1. Put on some positive, upbeat music and encourage the women to dance to it.

   ☞ *Women's music such as Holly Near, Sweet Honey in the Rock, Cris Williamson, etc. is very appropriate.*

2. End with women dancing together in a circle to the music.

VARIATION

■ This exercise works well as a closing activity for workshops.

■ You could adapt this activity to reinforce the self-esteem of individual participants when it seems appropriate. In this case, you would ask the woman to tell the group what she likes about herself and then have other members of the group provide her with her positive feedback.

34 GIFT SHARING

A fun closure activity in which group members make and give to each other gifts which symbolize what they appreciate about their fellow participants.

GOALS

To give and receive affection in the group.

To close the group.

TIME

2 hours

GROUP SIZE

On-going small group of no more than 12.

MATERIALS

Magic markers of many colors and a variety of other art materials.

PROCESS

Activity 1: Gift

☞ *This activity is most effective with a group that has been meeting for a while because members have experience with each other. It can also be used as a closure exercise for an on-going group.*

1. Start the exercise with the following instructions:
   - ➤ Each of us will have thirty minutes to find or make a gift for each member in the group.
   - ➤ You may use any resources you can find, including these art materials and the outside environment.
   - ➤ In deciding on the gifts to give, you may want to think about what you have appreciated about each person—what you like about her—then choose something that symbolizes this for you.

2. After thirty minutes, have each person take a turn to give her gifts to each group member and to share what she intended by the gift (if she wishes or if others want further clarification of its meaning).

3. Ask the group to discuss how members are feeling after completing this exercise.

VARIATION

■ If this is the last session of the group, you may want to examine how people feel about the group ending. Dealing with grief, if it is there, or any other feelings is important.

■ To simplify this exercise, have each group member tell the others what she would give them—a symbolic gift—rather than actually exchanging gifts, e.g., "I give to you a month to travel around the world so you can develop your adventurous spirit."

©1994 Whole Person Press 210 W Michigan Duluth MN 55802   (800) 247-6789

SELF-DISCOVERY READING LIST

Bass, Ellen and Laura Davis. *The Courage to Heal: A Guide for Women Survivors of Child Sexual Abuse.* New York: Perennial Library/Harper and Row, 1988.

Bepko, Claudia, ed. *Feminism and Addiction.* New York: Haworth Press, 1991.

Bepko, Claudia, and Joan Krestan. *Too Good for Her Own Good.* New York: Harper Collins, 1990.

Boston Lesbian Psychologies Collective. *Lesbian Psychologies.* Urbana, IL: U of Illinois Press, 1987.

Braud, Marjorie, ed. *Women, Power, and Therapy.* New York: Harrington Press, 1987.

Brody, Claire M., ed. *Women's Therapy Groups: Paradigms of Feminist Treatment.* New York: Springer, 1987.

Boyd, Julia. *In The Company of My Sisters: Black Women and Self-Esteem.* New York: Dutton, 1993.

Campling, Jo. *Images of Ourselves: Women and Disabilities Talking.* London: Rutledge, 1981.

Chesler, Phyllis. *Women and Madness.* New York: Harvest/HBJ, 1989.

Freedman, Rita. *Bodylove.* New York: Harper and Row, 1989.

Gilligan, Carol. *In a Different Voice: Psychological Theory and Women's Development.* Cambridge: Harvard University Press, 1993.

Hagan, Kay Leigh. *Internal Affairs: A Journal-keeping Workbook For Self-Intimacy.* San Francisco: Harper & Row, 1990.

Jack, Dana Crowley. *Silencing the Self: Women and Depression.* Cambridge, Massachusetts: Harvard University Press, 1991.

James, Muriel and Dorothy Jongeward. *Born To Win.* Reading, MA: Addison-Wesley Publishing Co., 1991.

Johnson, Karen. *Trusting Ourselves.* New York: Atlantic Monthly Press, 1991.

Jongeward, Dorothy and Dru Scott. *Women As Winners.* Reading, MA: Addison-Wesley Publishing Co., 1976.

©1994 Whole Person Press 210 W Michigan Duluth MN 55802   (800) 247-6789

Jones, Ann, and Susan Schechter. *When Love Goes Wrong: What To Do When You Can't Do Anything Right.* New York: HarperCollins, 1992.

Lerner, Harriet Goldhor. *The Dance of Anger.* New York: Harper & Row, 1985.

Mason, Marilyn. *Making Our Lives Our Own.* San Francisco: Harper, 1991.

Miller, Jean Baker. *Toward a New Psychology of Women.* Boston: Beacon Press, 1986.

Napier, Nancy. *Recreating Your Self.* New York: W.W. Norton, 1990.

Rush, Anne Kent. *Getting Clear.* New York: Random, 1973.

——. *Feminism As Therapy.* New York: Random, 1975.

Sanford, Linda T. and Mary Ellen Donovan. *Women and Self-Esteem: Understanding and Improving the Way We Think and Feel About Ourselves.* New York: Anchor/Doubleday, 1984.

Schaef, Anne Wilson. *Co-Dependence: Misunderstood—Mistreated.* San Francisco: Harper & Row, 1986.

Scarf, Maggie. *Intimate Partners: Patterns in Love and Marriage.* New York: Ballentine Books, 1987.

Steinem, Gloria. *Revolution From Within.* Boston: Little Brown and Company, 1992.

Usher, Jane. *Women's Madness.* Amherst, MA: U of Massachusetts Press, 1992.

Walsh, Mary. *The Psychology of Women.* New Haven: Yale UP, 1987.

Wisechild, Louise, ed. *She Who Was Lost Is Remembered: Healing From Incest Through Creativity.* Seattle: The Seal Press, 1991.

Women in Transition, Inc. *Women in Transition: A Feminist Handbook on Separation and Divorce.* New York: Charles Scribner's Sons, 1975.

Assertiveness Training

ASSERTIVENESS TRAINING

Assertiveness Training attracts a diverse group of women, all of whom have a strong desire to experience more personal power and increase their self-confidence. The reasons they come vary, but usually they want to:

● communicate and state wants more honestly and directly

● say "no" without feeling guilty

● express negative feelings, such as anger, without anxiety

● voice opinions and ideas freely and easily

● feel less anxious and more relaxed in uncomfortable and new situations

● gain respect from colleagues, doctors, salespeople, families, and others

● exercise personal rights without denying the rights of others

Regardless of individual circumstances, women have all experienced much the same social conditioning. Home, school, the media, and society in general still encourage women to act more passive, submissive, and nonassertive than men. Women are systematically reinforced to behave in self-denying ways. We please others and take care of their needs to the exclusion of our own. For example, we often agree to work on this charity or that committee when we have neither the time nor desire to serve. This "martyrdom" carries with it expectations of future rewards which often do not come and results in suppressed resentment and anger. The anger builds until it explodes, often at something completely unrelated. Guilt feelings often follow—reinforcing a negative self-image.

Women often believe that use of power will have negative consequences. Many women are concerned about being seen as too aggressive. We learn indirect methods such as cajoling and flattery to get what we want. These methods are not very successful and do not result in self-respect. For example, we play the "silent sufferer," hoping someone will guess what we need. Or we may use seductive and flirtatious behavior to get a nonsexual favor from a man.

We demonstrate low self-esteem over and over again by the qualifying apologetic language used at the beginning or ending of sentences: "I know this isn't important, but . . . ," "This is probably a stupid question, but . . . " "I'm sorry to take up so much of your time." Or we use such self-effacing phrases such as "It doesn't matter, whatever you want to do."

Assertiveness training provides an alternative to the games we have been taught, encouraging women to communicate directly and honestly. As we begin to develop a more adequate repertoire of assertive behavior—including language—we can begin to choose what for us are appropriate and healthy responses in a variety of situations. We become more ourselves. Handling situations more effectively results in increased self-esteem, more self-confidence, and less anxiety. In claiming our own needs we spare ourselves and others by taking responsibility for ourselves.

Assertiveness training involves learning and practicing new skills. It also reinforces the use of skills many women already possess—the ability to empathize with others, to sense what others are feeling, or to hear what others are saying, as well as the ability to phrase messages in a tactful, caring manner.

Women have been fearful of the labels of "bitch," "aggressive," and "butch" when demonstrating assertive behavior, although the same behavior in a man is seen as strong and competent. Assertiveness changes a woman's image and reputation. As more women become assertive the view of what is appropriate behavior for women will improve.

NOTES TO FACILITATORS:

Choice is an essential element to emphasize when leading assertiveness training groups. You will be helping women gain assertiveness skills which they can then decide to use or not. Encourage each person to behave in the way that feels best for them.

Women are often not conscious of using qualifying or apologetic language. In a nonjudgmental and caring way, point out the language when you hear it. As they become more conscious of what they are saying, eventually they will notice and correct it.

Women are worried about what will happen if they act assertively. Many in assertiveness groups mention their worst fears but none of the positive possibilities. When this happens, it is important to encourage the discussion of the possible positive consequences. To illustrate, in a recent group one person kept talking about all the disastrous consequences if she disagreed with her boss. He would regard her as aggressive, insubordinate, and unfeminine; she would thus lose her job. She did not present the other possibilities: that he would feel more respect for her, she might get a

©1994 Whole Person Press 210 W Michigan Duluth MN 55802   (800) 247-6789

promotion, and in the end, and most importantly, she would feel better about herself. Point out that assertive behavior may not produce wished-for-responses, nevertheless it makes us feel better about ourselves.

Some feel reluctant and fearful to give up old behavior patterns. You will find as you facilitate the workshop (and support group) that people will challenge you, debating whether assertiveness will work in their particular situations. Rather than getting into a long discussion or becoming defensive, ask the person to role-play the situation with you (you play her and she plays the difficult party). This is usually effective. It demonstrates the technique you are talking about, plus you are modeling risk taking and the use of assertiveness skills. Role-playing is more valuable and interesting to others in the group than a dialogue between the two of you.

THE STRUCTURE OF THIS SECTION:

This section of the book is actually divided into two separate elements, an **Assertiveness Workshop** (exercises 35 through 44) and an **Assertiveness Support Group** (exercises 45 through 48).

THE ASSERTIVENESS WORKSHOP:

Objectives:

1. To look at the difference between assertive, nonassertive, and aggressive behavior.

2. To locate some of the areas in our lives in which we feel we either lack assertiveness or "come on too strong."

3. To examine some of the ways we keep ourselves from expressing our needs, wants, opinions, or feelings.

4. To practice new ways of handling those situations that we find difficult or uncomfortable.

Materials

Easels and easel paper; magic markers; masking tape; paper; pencils.

Time

A one day workshop (seven to eight hours), followed by an on-going support group meeting weekly for four to five weeks, two-and-one-half hours each week. (While this section is designed as a day long workshop, you can revise it to use with a continuing group which meets weekly.)

Group Size

For the workshop, thirty persons are manageable if they are divided into three small groups for the majority of the skill practices, with one or two facilitators for each group. Theory presentations and some skill work will be conducted in the large group and in subgroups.

THE ASSERTIVENESS SUPPORT GROUP

A support group helps provide necessary reinforcement for new behavior. Learning new skills involves practice and repractice, plus encouragement in the form of positive strokes from self and others.

Therefore, begin each support group session with "success" time, each person describing the positive assertions she made during the week. Time can also be given to the difficulties each encountered.

The support group should be no larger than twelve persons with one or two facilitators. Members should stay in the same group throughout the sessions.

In the support session, the main learning method is role-playing. (Follow the guidelines in the workshop section.) Exercises 45 through 48, in addition to role-playing, are appropriate to use in a support group.

35 GROUP INTRODUCTIONS

Workshop goals, methods, and roles are discussed and guidelines developed after participants are introduced to the concept of assertiveness.

GOALS

To introduce the methods and guidelines for the workshop.

To get acquainted by identifying a situation in which each person is assertive.

TIME

30 minutes

MATERIALS

None.

PROCESS

Activity 1: Get Acquainted

1. Start with the following chalktalk:
   - For many of us, asking for what we want, saying no to what we do not want, dealing with conflict, and expressing our feelings directly are experiences often accompanied by feelings of anxiety, inadequacy, and guilt.
   - In this workshop we will have the opportunity:
     - to look at the difference between assertive, passive, and aggressive behavior;
     - to locate some of the areas in our lives in which we feel we either lack assertiveness or "come on too strong;"
     - to examine some of the ways we keep ourselves from expressing our needs, wants, opinions, or feelings;
     - to practice new ways of handling those situations which we find difficult or uncomfortable.
   - Following this workshop, you will probably feel better about yourself and find you have increased your ability to communicate more powerfully.

● Let's begin with each of us saying our name and one area in our life in which we already feel assertive. I will begin . . .

☞ *Go around the group until all have shared.*

Workshop Overview

1. Explain the facilitators' roles, the schedule, and the methods to be used.

2. Ask for any questions about the workshop.

3. Develop guidelines with group input for how the group would like to work together (e.g., confidentiality, openness, honesty, risk taking, etc.) Record these guidelines on the easel chart and refine them until all group members agree to follow them.

VARIATION

■ For an alternative way to have participants introduce themselves in Activity 1, ask each member to share one positive aspect and one negative aspect concerning assertiveness in her life.

36 LABELS

Participants brainstorm labels for aggressive and passive men and women and discuss what these labels imply about acceptable behavior for both genders.

GOALS

To discover the stereotypes participants hold about assertive and non-assertive male and female behavior.

To begin to understand how the culture has influenced women's behavior and attitudes about assertiveness.

TIME

20 minutes

MATERIALS

Paper and pencils.

PROCESS

Activity 1: Stereotypical Labels

1. Inform participants that they are going to spend a short time exploring their own assertive attitudes and our culture's assumptions about women's and men's behavior.

2. Distribute paper and pencils and ask participants to write all the words that come to them when they hear the terms below. They are not to evaluate or screen out words, just put down the first ones they think of. State each term, allow one minute for writing, then state the next. The terms are:

   ● nonassertive woman

   ● nonassertive man

   ● aggressive woman

   ● aggressive man

3. Instruct participants to circle the words or phrases in each list that are positive and look for any trends or patterns in the lists.

4. Form small groups of eight to ten and assign a facilitator to each group.

5. Have facilitators ask the participants to share what they wrote under each term.

   ☞ *You may want to record these on an easel chart.*

6. Provide time for the small groups to discuss the labels with these questions in mind:

   ✔ What do the words you listed imply about acceptable behavior for men and women? (e.g., societal approval of aggressive males and passive females.)

   ✔ Have any of these societal norms or stereotypes influenced your behavior? If so, in what ways?

7. Tell participants that in the next exercise they will have an opportunity to explore culture's messages in a more personal way.

VARIATION

■ In *Step 2*, instead of having participants write their individual responses, have the group brainstorm responses and record them on the easel chart.

©1994 Whole Person Press 210 W Michigan Duluth MN 55802   (800) 247-6789

37 ASSERTIVENESS MESSAGES

Participants examine how they learned to be assertive, passive, or aggressive and later identify what they most want to work on during this workshop.

GOALS

To examine the ways participants have learned to become assertive or nonassertive.

To examine how messages have influenced their present behavior.

To begin to think about changing destructive messages and behaviors.

TIME

45 minutes

MATERIALS

Exploring Messages About Assertiveness worksheet.

PROCESS

Activity 1: Exploring Messages

1. Distribute the worksheet and instruct each person to take five minutes and answer the questions.

2. Call time when most are done and have them form trios.

3. Ask participants to disclose the messages they received and the decisions they made.

4. After twenty minutes, reconvene the large group and invite participants to voice any discoveries they have made.

Activity 2: Moving Beyond Our Socialization

1. Illustrate through a brief lecture the socialization of women and the need for assertiveness training. (If need be, use the books suggested on the Assertiveness Training Reading List as additional resources.)

2. Ask participants to share what kinds of behaviors they would like to work on and change during this workshop.

EXPLORING MESSAGES ABOUT ASSERTIVENESS

1. How did your family deal with conflict? Was there a difference
   between how the women and the men handled conflict?

2. What messages did your family give you about getting what you
   wanted? (list them) Is there one major theme in these messages? If
   so, what is it?

3. Place a check mark (✔) next to any of the messages or ways of
   handling conflict that encourage non-assertive or indirect behavior,
   an "X" next to those that encourage aggressive and attacking
   behavior, and a star (*) next to those that encourage assertive and
   appropriate behavior.

4. What decisions did you make about ways to get what you wanted?
   Do you still act on these decisions? If so, what are the payoffs for
   these decisions? The costs?

©1994 Whole Person Press 210 W Michigan Duluth MN 55802   (800) 247-6789

38 DEFINITIONS

This fun activity fully engages participants and increases their understanding of the differences between assertive, passive, and aggressive behavior.

GOALS

To develop a greater understanding of the differences between assertive, nonassertive, and aggressive behavior in various situations.

To begin to get comfortable with role-playing and with the group members.

TIME

1 hour

MATERIALS

Typical Characteristics worksheets; 3 cardboard signs, one reading "Assertive," the second "Passive," and the third "Aggressive."

PROCESS

Defining Activity

1. Present each person with a copy of the worksheet and discuss it with the group.

    ☞ *Make sure to give some examples in each category that are appropriate to the group.*

2. Divide the large group into three equal groups. Distribute a different behavior sign to each group.

3. Give the following directions:

    ➤ I will read a situation.

    ➤ Each group's task is to decide how the situation should be played according to the behavior sign the group is given, using your worksheet as a guide.

    ➤ Choose one person to act out that particular behavior in a role-play.

4. Read the first situation. Choose one from the suggested situations below or develop your own.

©1994 Whole Person Press 210 W Michigan Duluth MN 55802   (800) 247-6789

☞ *These are only suggestions. It is best to develop typical scenarios which are custom tailored to the group you are working with.*

● You are at a party, talking with a man who is interested in having a close relationship with you. You do not want to pursue any relationship with him. You say and do . . .

● At the office your co-worker asks you to write a report that is her responsibility. It's at the end of the day and you will either have to stay late or take it home to finish it, as she wants it done by tomorrow morning. You say and do . . .

● You are in a car pool. Today you asked Tony, the driver, to be on time because you have an important meeting at 9 a.m. about a promotion you may get. It takes thirty minutes to get to the office. Tony arrives at 8:45 a.m. You say and do . . .

5. After about five minutes, call time. Announce that one of the facilitators will play the other character in the situation. Name the first behavior to be demonstrated and ask the person chosen to play that behavior to come forward and have them take a new name for the role-play. (Save the assertive scene for last.) After each behavior is presented in a role-play, ask each person how she felt in the scene. Ask for input from the group about behavior they observed that fits the role they were to play and then move to the next behavior role-play.

6. After all three behaviors have been played, discuss the differences.

7. Read the next situation and proceed as above.

☞ *Generally it is helpful to give each group the opportunity to work on all three behavior roles. However, in some groups one situation role-played with all three behaviors is enough for participants' understanding. Use your own judgment.*

8. Thank the role-players for their participation and risk taking.

VARIATION

■ Before starting the exercise, ask participants to write a scenario they would like to handle more assertively. Choose several that fit the group and can be easily role-played for demonstration.

TYPICAL CHARACTERISTICS

OF NONASSERTIVE, AGGRESSIVE, AND ASSERTIVE PEOPLE

Behavior	Nonassertive	Aggressive	Assertive
Characteristics	lets others make her decisions for her, doesn't express feelings, ideas, wants, puts self down, in a conflict runs away or gives in, uses apologetic words, hedges, uses an indirect manner (hoping someone will guess what she wants), cries, pleads, is hesitant, has downcast eyes.	is inappropriately honest, puts others down, ignores rights of others, dominates, chooses for others, attacks and blames, overreacts in situations, uses "loaded" and superior words, is sarcastic, loud, makes rigid demands, points finger	is appropriately honest, expresses wants and feelings directly, chooses for herself, is empathetic, evaluates and acts, is spontaneous, exercises her personal rights and respects rights of others, uses objective words, listens, makes direct eye contact, has firm and warm voice, uses "I" statements.
Reasons	to avoid conflict and unpleasant, risky situations.	to express hostility and anger, to achieve objectives (in the short run at least).	to achieve objectives, to have positive feelings about herself.
Feelings about self that accompany this behavior	low self-confidence and low self-esteem, hurt, helpless, anxious, powerless, possibly resentful and angry (at a later time), guilty, inhibited.	high or low self-esteem, hostile, superior, righteous, alienated, defensive, frustrated, bitter, tense.	self-respect, confident, self-sufficient, powerful, relaxed.
Feelings of others when a person engages in this behavior	guilty, angry, disrespectful, irritated, frustrated, superior.	hurt, humiliated, defensive, vengeful, angry.	respectful, respected, threatened (occasionally)

39 PERSONAL BILL OF RIGHTS

Each participant develops a list of rights she expects to have and begins to make the connection between rights and assertive behavior.

GOALS

To understand the connection between rights and assertive behavior.

To determine the rights each woman wants to have in her life.

TIME

20 minutes

MATERIALS

Pencils; **My Personal Bill of Rights** worksheet.

PROCESS

Activity 1: Rights

1. Introduce this activity by saying:
   - All of us have personal rights in life. Many times we ignore, or do not acknowledge, what our rights are.
   - This in turn prevents us from asserting ourselves to get what we want and usually results in training others to mistreat us.
   - Thus, it's important to determine and stand up for our rights, recognizing that others also have rights.

2. Distribute the worksheets and pencils and ask participants to write down the rights they would like to have for themselves. It is helpful to give one or two examples. Some rights often mentioned by group members:
   - The right to be my own judge of what I say, think, or feel.
   - The right to say no without feeling guilty.
   - The right to make mistakes.
   - The right to be treated with respect.
   - The right to privacy and to have time alone.

- The right to feel and express anger.
- The right to be independent.
- The right to reject culturally imposed stereotypes.

3. Invite the members to express some of their rights and record them on the easel. Tape up the easel sheet on the wall to remind everyone of rights they may want to claim for themselves.

4. Segue into the next activity by telling them they will now begin to practice some assertive skills.

VARIATIONS

■ If you are working with a specific occupational group (i.e., nurses, engineers, secretaries, law students), have participants work as a group to develop a bill of rights for their occupation.

■ Have each participant write her personal bill of rights on an easel sheet and post it on a wall as a public reminder of what she wants. It can also be referred to during her work on specific situations throughout the workshop.

MY PERSONAL BILL OF RIGHTS

1.

2.

3.

4.

5.

6.

7.

8.

9.

10.

11.

12.

40 ASSERTIVE TALK

Participants practice conversation skills, especially how to initiate conversations and learn more about someone, and the art of self-disclosure.

GOALS

To learn to initiate conversation with others.

To practice the skill of self-disclosure.

TIME

45 minutes

MATERIALS

None.

PROCESS

Activity 1: Introduction to Conversation Skills

1. Introduce the activity with the following chalktalk:
   - Practicing new behavior patterns is the key to developing assertiveness.
   - We are going to start with a basic skill, that of initiating and responding to conversation with another person.

2. Present members with some conversational suggestions (prepared ahead of time on easel paper):
   - ✔ Use the "free" information the other person gives you to learn more about her. It can be something she's wearing, something you have seen her do or say. (e.g., "I really like that unusual ring you are wearing. What's the story behind it?")
   - ✔ Ask open-ended questions, such as "how, what, when, where." Do not ask "why" questions which tend to create defensiveness in the other.
   - ✔ Share your initial feelings about the person. (e.g., "Ever since you introduced yourself by saying that you are assertive in your relationships with men, I have felt curious about you and have wanted to talk with you.")

✔ Disclose some things about yourself by giving your opinions, thoughts, feelings, wants, and/or fears.

Activity 2: Assertive Talk

1. Divide the group in half, each half remaining opposite each other but in the same room.

2. Give the following directions to members of the group on your right:

   ➤ Each of you is to choose one person from the group on my left who you would like to know better or about whom you are curious.

   ➤ When you have chosen someone, initiate a conversation with her, practicing the conversation skills.

3. After five minutes, tell the pairs to talk with each other about the experience, discussing when they felt comfortable and uncomfortable in the conversation.

   ☞ *The goal is to become comfortable in both initiating and pursuing a conversation, as well as disclosing oneself.*

4. Repeat the exercise. This time the opposite group chooses the partner and initiates the conversation, practicing the conversation skills.

5. Bring the group back together and encourage members to share anything they learned from the experience.

VARIATION

■ In Activity 1, facilitators could demonstrate the use of conversation skills through a prepared role-play.

41 SAYING "NO"

Using guidelines for saying "no" assertively, participants identify and then role-play one of their difficult "no" situations, exploring how to be assertive in that situation.

GOALS

To understand the skills involved in saying "no."

To practice saying "no" in various situations.

TIME

1 ½ hours

MATERIALS

Guidelines for Saying "No" worksheet; **Difficult Situations** worksheet.

PROCESS

Activity 1: Skill Guidelines

1. Begin with the following chalktalk:

   ● The next skill we will work on is saying "no."

   ● Many women have difficulty saying "no" to requests. Our socialization teaches us to be friendly and cooperative, sometimes at the expense of our own wishes.

   ● Thus, we often find ourselves saying yes to others, but later regretting it, feeling resentful that we have been pressured. On the other hand, if we say no, we feel guilty.

   ● It is a skill to tell others we don't want to do something, refusing in a way that doesn't hurt a relationship but enhances it.

2. Distribute the **Guidelines for Saying "No"** worksheet and elaborate on each guideline:

   ● Say "no" with strength and without getting upset.

   ● Do not go into long explanations or rationalizations for saying "no." This leads the other person to think you're not serious, and he or she will probably continue to try to get you to change your weak "no" to a "yes."

- Say "I won't" rather than "I can't." "Won't" implies the decision is your choice and firm; "can't" indicates outside forces are influencing the decision.

- Do not apologize, saying "I'm sorry but . . . "

- Use the "broken record" technique which is simply saying "no" over and over again in a calm voice without being diverted to side issues until the person hears the message. It also helps to be empathetic, letting the other person know you understand how she is feeling, e.g., "I hear how upset you feel, but I do not want to . . . "

Activity 2: Practice Saying "No"

1. Distribute the **Difficult Situations** worksheet and ask each participant to jot down or think of two situations in which she has difficulty saying "no."

2. Divide the group into two or three subgroups and have them move to separate areas of the room.

3. Direct members to describe their situations and role-play saying "no" in that situation.

   ☞ *Let each person practice saying "no" with another member playing the other party. The others coach the one practicing. All give feedback to her after the role-play. The facilitator's role is to move from group to group, helping those who want it.*

4. Reconvene the large group. Start a discussion of the difficulties and advantages they found using the following questions:

   ✔ How did you feel when you said no?

   ✔ How did you feel when no was said to you?

   ✔ What situations were the easiest to say no to? The most difficult?

VARIATION

■ You could adjust Activity 2 to two rounds: in the first round each person presents her easiest situation. Have them choose a more difficult situation for the second round. Two rounds give participants more time to develop their skills.

GUIDELINES FOR SAYING "NO"

1. Say "no" with strength and without getting upset.

2. Do not go into long explanations or rationalizations for saying no. This leads the other person to think you are not serious and he or she will probably continue to try to get you to change your weak "no" to a "yes."

3. Say "I won't" rather than "I can't." "Won't" implies the decision is your choice and firm; "can't" indicates outside forces are influencing the decision.

4. Do not apologize, saying "I'm sorry, but. . . ."

5. Use the "broken record" technique, which is simply saying "no" over and over again in a calm voice without being diverted to side issues until the person hears the message. It also helps to be empathetic, letting the other person know you understand how he or she is feeling, e.g., "I hear how upset you feel, but I do not want to . . ."

DIFFICULT SITUATIONS

Instructions: Describe one or two situations in which you have
          difficulty saying "no."

1.

2.

42 ANXIETY AND RELAXATION

In small groups, participants identify anxious situations and explore how to relax in those stressful times.

GOALS

To identify relaxation as an important step in reducing anxiety, which blocks assertiveness.

To discuss anxious situations and explore how to relax in those situations.

TIME

30 minutes

MATERIALS

Anxious Situations worksheets.

PROCESS

Activity 1: Body Cues

1. Form small groups.

    ☞ *Preselect these groups for balance.*

2. In each small group, engage the members in a discussion of what body cues they have when they are feeling anxious or uptight, (e.g., headache, stomach pains, heart pounding, blushing, looking down, etc.).

3. Ask them to name ways they use to relax.

    ☞ *The point is to give the women more options of how they might relax in different situations.*

Activity 2: Anxious Situations

1. Distribute the worksheet and instruct participants to list situations that create anxious feelings in themselves.

2. Have participants number the situations in order from least anxiety provoking to most anxiety provoking.

3. Have participants describe their situations to their small groups and discuss how they might relax more in each situation.

VARIATION

■ Instead of preselecting small groups, have participants go through a self-select process (this presents a great opportunity to process any anxiety and assertiveness in a real life process).

ANXIOUS SITUATIONS

____ 1.

____ 2.

____ 3.

____ 4.

____ 5.

____ 6.

____ 7.

____ 8.

43 DIFFICULT SITUATIONS

The group videotapes role-play situations to help each participant develop ways to handle specific situations more assertively.

GOALS

To explore new ways to handle difficult/uncomfortable situations.

To practice assertiveness skills.

TIME

4 hours

MATERIALS

Video camera and monitor; VCR (one set for each small group).

PROCESS

Activity 1: Assertive Skill Practice

1. Present the goals and explain to participants that they will practice assertiveness skills by role-playing situations that will be videotaped.

2. Form small groups and give members time to express any feelings they have about taking part in role-plays and being videotaped, e.g., embarrassment, fear, etc.

3. Ask each person to think of a situation they would like to handle more assertively and would be willing to work on today. Give them a few minutes to identify that situation.

4. One at a time, role-play these situations, following this procedure:

   a. First, ask for a volunteer and have her describe the situation, giving enough information so it is clear, but not going into its history in great detail. Make certain she states her goal—what she wants out of the interaction—very specifically.

   b. Then have her invite someone to work with her while the rest of the group members observe. Allow time for this person to ask questions about the role she is to play.

c. Start the role-play with the person involved in the situation playing herself as she would like to be; videotape the role-play.

d. Stop when you have enough material to explore, and ask each role-player how she is feeling.

e. Play back the video, stopping at key points for discussion.

f. Give feedback to the person who initiated the role-play.

g. Replay the situation until the person is satisfied with how she can handle this situation in the future.

   ☞ *Usually through this rehearsal, an assertive solution is discovered. Role-plays help a woman see that usually nothing disastrous happens when she is assertive. She gains confidence as she learns new skills and options for handling situations.*

5. Continue as above, giving an opportunity for each person to role-play their situation.

Closure

1. Lead a group discussion about what participants learned from their role-play and from observing others.

2. Encourage them to continue to use and practice these new skills.

VARIATION

■ It is possible to conduct Activity 1 without videotaping. However, learning will be greatly enhanced when you use videotaping. If you do not use the video, this exercise will take about two hours.

©1994 Whole Person Press 210 W Michigan Duluth MN 55802   (800) 247-6789

44 CLOSURE AND EVALUATION

In this closing activity, members receive compliments from the group, identify what they have learned, and give feedback about the experience.

GOALS

To practice the skill of accepting compliments.

To close the group and summarize what has been learned.

To evaluate the workshop.

TIME

1 hour

MATERIALS

None

PROCESS

Activity 1: Accepting Compliments

1. Share the objectives for this session.

2. Form small groups and give the following directions:

   ➤ We are going to spend the next few minutes practicing the skill of accepting compliments.

   ➤ The procedure will be to go around the group, taking a few minutes to tell each person what we have appreciated or liked about her participation in the workshop.

   ➤ When it is your turn to receive appreciations or compliments, acknowledge them in some way; do not discount or deny them. Be sincere and honest when you give compliments to others.

   ➤ Who would like to be first to hear compliments?

3. When everyone has had a turn, take a few minutes to explore how it felt to give and receive compliments.

Closure

1. Reassemble the large group and form small groups of four to five members using participants from each of the previous small groups.

2. Ask them to summarize what they have learned from the workshop and record their responses on an easel sheet.

3. After fifteen minutes, ask them to report what they learned to the group.

Workshop Evaluation

1. Conduct an evaluation of the workshop by first asking for any verbal feedback.

2. Distribute a written evaluation. (If you want this information.)

Support Group/Follow-up

☞ *This is the final portion of the Assertiveness Training Workshop. It is designed to help you set up an Assertiveness Support Group for members of the workshop. Use the following five exercises (45–48) for the* **Assertiveness Support Groups**. *See page 135 for information on establishing support groups and using those exercises.*

1. Invite participants to join you in an on-going assertiveness support group.

2. Present details of the support group—what time it will be meeting, where, etc.

3. Tell the participants not to put pressure on themselves to go out and become assertive overnight. Some points you might make include:

   ● Use less anxious situations in your first attempt to be assertive.

   ● Give yourself a reward when you try some new behavior whether you were successful or not.

   ● Remember that change takes time. The first step is not necessarily being assertive but noticing your nonassertiveness immediately after it occurs. Reward yourself for noticing.

VARIATION

■ You may wish to conduct Activity 1 as a large group if you have fewer than fifteen participants.

©1994 Whole Person Press 210 W Michigan Duluth MN 55802   (800) 247-6789

45 MAKING REQUESTS

Group members practice the skill of making requests by asking for what they want from others and role-playing specific scenarios.

GOALS

To become more comfortable making requests of others.

To practice asking what we want from others.

TIME

30 minutes to 4 hours, depending on the size of the group

MATERIALS

None.

PROCESS

☞ *Before you use this exercise and exercises 46–48, be sure to read "Assertiveness Support Groups" on page 135. The information in that passage will help you establish an effective support group.*

Introduction

1. Introduce the exercise with the following chalktalk:
   - There are several reasons that we don't get what we want: often we act as if we will easily back off our requests, we get caught up in side issues brought up by others, or we begin to act like we should not have brought up the request in the first place.
   - Our fear of rejection often prevents us from asking for things. We fail to realize that the other person can say "no" and that does not necessarily mean they don't like us—and they may also say "yes." We'll never know unless we ask.
   - In this session each of us will have the opportunity to ask a favor or make a request for something we want in this group.
2. Instruct members to look around the group and identify some things they want from other members or from the whole group.

3. After two or three minutes, give participants the opportunity to go to several others in the group and try to get what they want.

4. After fifteen to thirty minutes (whenever most seem done) discuss this experience. Ask group members if they had any requests or wants that they censored. Examine together the fears or reasons for not bringing these up.

Activity 1: Individual Scenarios

1. Allow time for individuals who want to practice handling making requests of others in their life.

2. Follow the role-play process in Exercise 43, **Difficult Situations**, without using the videotaping.

VARIATION

■ During the Introduction activity, have each participant ask for what they want from other members of the group and then discuss the presentation and reaction to each request.

46 HANDLING CRITICISM

Participants practice giving and receiving negative feedback in a variety of ways using specific guidelines provided by the trainer.

GOALS

To become more comfortable receiving and giving criticism.

To explore ways to respond to criticism.

To practice responding assertively to criticism.

TIME

2 hours

MATERIALS

Ways to Respond to Criticism worksheet; **Feedback Criteria** worksheet.

PROCESS

Activity 1: Ways to Respond to Criticism

1. Begin this exercise with the following chalktalk:
   - Many of us fear criticism. When others criticize us we do not respond assertively; instead we feel defensive, anxious, rejected, and/or hurt.
   - It is equally difficult for us to give negative impressions or criticisms as we fear we will hurt the other person or perhaps be rejected by them.
   - What we fail to think about is the greater respect from others we may gain by being more assertive in giving and receiving criticism. In addition we will like and respect ourselves.
   - In this session you will have an opportunity to practice both responding assertively to criticism and giving criticism to others.

2. Distribute the **Ways to Respond to Criticism** worksheet and discuss each item.

3. In order to demonstrate some of these responses to criticism, request some negative feedback or criticism from the group members. Tell them it can be "real" or "made-up" criticism. After responding to each critical comment, explain what method you used and what you were feeling.

Activity 2: Criticism Practice

1. Instruct the group members to work in pairs, taking turns giving criticism and responding assertively to it, practicing some of the tactics found on the **Ways to Respond to Criticism** worksheet.

2. After about five to seven minutes, reassemble the group and ask the pairs to discuss what happened.

3. Give the following directions for the next activity:

   ➤ Now you will have an opportunity to practice giving negative feedback or reservations to each person in the group.

   ➤ Someone will volunteer to start and will go around the group to each person one at a time, sharing their negative feedback.

   ☞ *Proceeding at this point depends on how the participants react to the directions. Only proceed if a majority of participants wish to continue, and allow those that do not to excuse themselves for the remainder of this activity.*

4. Check with the group members to see if they wish to participate in this process. If they do, distribute the **Feedback Criteria** worksheet and review its guidelines.

5. If they agree to participate, give them the following directions:

   ➤ I will ask for a volunteer and have her go to each person, first asking the person if she wants to hear any reservations or negative impressions.

   ➤ If she does, the volunteer gives feedback and listens to her response.

   ➤ We will continue this process until each of you has had an opportunity to receive negative feedback.

6. When the volunteer has gone around the group, allow time for the group members to reflect upon the experience.

7. Move on to the next person who would like to practice giving negative feedback. Continue this process until all who want to participate have had the opportunity.

   ☞ *Rationale: The whole process of hearing and learning how to respond assertively to criticism or negative feedback makes us more immune to devastation and builds self confidence (if this is done in a climate of goodwill).*

8. Encourage participants to summarize what they learned from this experience.

WAYS TO RESPOND TO CRITICISM

1. Agree with it. ("I also do not like it when I do that.")

2. Request more information about what the person means ("Could you be more specific? What about my being quiet bothers you?")

3. Acknowledge that you heard it and that you disagree ("What I hear you saying is that you think I have given too many suggestions in the role-plays. Although I can understand how you might feel that way, I feel my contributions have been valuable and I will continue offering them.")

4. Express what you are feeling, having heard the feedback. ("I am feeling upset. It wasn't my intention to avoid you.")

5. Hear the feedback and deal with the issue it raises later. ("You sound angry about last night's meeting. I appreciate your telling me. Let's discuss it further after dinner.")

©1994 Whole Person Press 210 W Michigan Duluth MN 55802   (800) 247-6789

FEEDBACK CRITERIA

To be effective, feedback should be:

1. **Descriptive (NOT evaluative):** Describe the behavior, do not judge it or respond to personality and assumed motivation. Do not use right/wrong language, e.g., "Janet, I notice that you are going braless these days," not, "Janet, what are you trying to prove not wearing a bra?"

2. **Specific (instead of general):** Talk about a specific type of behavior, e.g., "When you started talking to Rona while I was crying, I felt you did not care about me," not "You are very inconsiderate and cold."

3. **Useable:** Only deal with that which a person can do something about; not, "I do not like the shape of your face."

4. **Requested:** Feedback is heard most easily when it is asked for by the other person. There is also the option of asking a person if they want to hear some feedback you wish to offer.

5. **Timely:** Feedback is best when you give it as soon after the action or behavior as possible and appropriate.

An effective rule is to ask another person to repeat back in her own words what she heard you say, especially in a conflict situation. In that way, you have an opportunity to clear up any misunderstandings right on the spot.

©1994 Whole Person Press 210 W Michigan Duluth MN 55802   (800) 247-6789

47 EXPRESSING ANGER

After examining the socialization messages women receive about anger, participants explore how to express their anger in healthy ways.

GOALS

To learn how women often internalize anger.

To legitimize the expression of anger.

To provide assertive ways to express anger.

TIME

2 hours

MATERIALS

Anger Situations worksheet.

PROCESS

Activity 1: Messages About Anger

1. Announce the topic and invite the group to call out responses to the following four open-ended sentences (record answers on the easel):

   ● I express my anger indirectly by . . . (e.g., being silent, complaining to others about the "offender.")

   ● I internalize my anger by . . . (e.g., being depressed, getting a headache.)

   ● If I express my anger directly, I fear . . . (e.g., I would be called a bitch, be seen as castrating, unlikable.)

   ● I feel angry when others . . .

2. Initiate a discussion of how these answers reflect the socialization messages and training we have received about getting angry. You might say:

   ● We have been told not to express anger by our culture. Women who show anger are called "bitchy" and "masculine."

   ● In fact, this socialization may be so complete, we are completely unaware that we have feelings of irritation or anger.

- If we are taught not to express these feelings overtly, we soon learn to express them indirectly or turn the anger against ourselves, most often by getting depressed. For example, we may overeat and then feel depressed.

- Let's discuss the socialization messages you see in the answers we have given to those four questions.

Activity 2: Healthy Anger

1. Distribute the **Anger Situations** worksheet and ask participants to:

   ➤ Think of a specific situation or incident in which you have felt irritated or angry but have not expressed these feelings directly.

   ➤ Use the questions found on the worksheet to reflect on that incident.

   ➤ Write down your answers.

2. Give them five minutes to fill out the handout.

3. After about five minutes, present some points about anger such as:

   ➤ Remind yourself anger is a healthy, normal, and real emotion.

   ➤ Be congruent: your words, voice, and facial expressions should match (e.g., don't smile when you say you are angry).

   ➤ Express your anger directly and with "I" messages, e.g. "I feel very angry right now." "I am so mad, I feel like hitting you." Do not use "you" messages which tend to blame and put the other on the defensive, e.g., "You make me so mad," "You are so inconsiderate."

   ➤ Identify the source of your anger and why you are angry.

   ➤ Make a direct request—what change do you want in the future?

4. Divide the group in half. Explain:

   ➤ As you can see, it is important for our own emotional health for us to learn how to express our anger assertively.

   ➤ In your subgroup, take turns describing the situation you just spent time thinking and writing about.

   ➤ After that, you will each have a chance to role-play your situation, practicing expressing your angry feelings directly.

5. Role-plays are conducted with those members who want to work on their anger. After each role-play allow time for the group members to give feedback.

6. Reconvene the large group and review how each participant felt in the "anger" role-plays and what they learned.

> ☞ *Alert the group members that once they begin to voice anger, they may find themselves angry much of the time. This may last for a while (until some of the stored up anger has been released). Then they can begin to express anger when they feel it and when it is appropriate to the situation.*

VARIATIONS

■ An alternative approach to Activity 1 is to have each member complete the four sentences individually with the rest of the group listening.

■ If some group members are uncomfortable expressing anger, have them pretend to be an animal who is angry and, as a group, move about the room for five minutes behaving like that angry animal. This should help release repressed energy and can be lots of fun. Works best if used after Activity 1.

ANGER SITUATIONS

1. To whom and toward what behavior or action was your anger directed?

2. What did you actually do and say?

3. What did you want to do and say?

4. What were your fears behind what you wanted to do and say?

48 APPRECIATING OURSELVES

In this closing activity, each participant gives a presentation about her own positive aspects and then practices receiving honest expressions of appreciation about herself.

GOALS

To give practice in acknowledging good things about themselves.

To practice giving and receiving honest expressions of appreciation.

To close the group.

TIME

1 ½ hours

MATERIALS

None.

PROCESS

Activity 1: Acknowledging Ourselves

1. Begin with the following chalktalk:
   - To end the group, let's work on one more skill: acknowledging and accepting our positive qualities.
   - Many women have been taught to not mention their positive qualities or assets—the modest and humble woman is the ideal model presented to us. Along with this message society gives us another: don't acknowledge compliments from others.
   - Thus, if someone compliments me on the good job I have done in organizing the conference, I say: "Oh, it was nothing, anyone could have done it." By this type of comment we discount ourselves and the other person.
   - An assertive response would be either to accept the compliment ("Thank you") or to disclose something about yourself as you accept it ("Thank you, Mary. I worked very hard on putting together the best conference possible. I'm glad you liked it. I did too. I feel good that you took the time to let me know your feelings.")

- It is healthy to take pride in your accomplishments.

2. Discuss the activity, covering these points:

   ➤ First, you will give a one to two minute talk about the positive things you like about yourself. Do not mention any negative qualities.

   ➤ Time will then be given to those in the group who want to tell you what they like about you. Accept the compliments; do not discount them.

   ☞ *It is an anxiety-producing situation for many women to speak positively about themselves, but it is also a reinforcing and positive experience to do this and to receive positive feedback. Sometimes women also give "false" compliments in an attempt to make someone feel better or to hide negative feelings. One purpose of this activity is to encourage them to share positive feelings only if they are sincere.*

3. Conduct the activity with each person, giving time for reflection after each person has received positive feedback from the group members.

Group Closure

1. Have participants stand and form a tight circle.

2. Ask each member to say

   - how she is feeling about the group ending, and

   - what the group has meant to her.

3. End with a circle hug.

©1994 Whole Person Press 210 W Michigan Duluth MN 55802   (800) 247-6789

ASSERTIVENESS READING LIST

Alberti, R.E., and M.L. Emmons. *Stand Up, Speak Out, Talk Back.* New York: Pocket Books, 1970.

——. *Your Perfect Right.* San Luis Obispo: Impact, 1970.

Austin, Nancy and Stanley Phelps. *The Assertive Woman.* San Suis Obispo: Impact, 1992.

Bach, George and Herb Goldberg. *Creative Aggression.* New York: Avon Books, 1974.

Bach, George and Peter Wyden. *The Intimate Enemy.* New York: Avon Books, 1968.

Baer, Jean. *How to be an Assertive Woman.* New York: Penguin Books, 1976.

Barreca, Regina. *They Used to Call Me Snow White . . . But I Drifted.* New York: Penguin Books, 1991.

Bloom, Lynn, Karen Coburn, and Joan Pearlman. *The New Assertive Woman.* New York: Delacorte Press, 1975.

Butler, Pamela. *Self-Assertion for Women.* New York: HarperCollins, 1992.

Elgin, Suzette Haden. *Genderspeak.* Boston: John Wiley, 1993.

Hall, Lindsey and Leigh Cohen. *Self-Esteem: Tools for Recovery.* Gurze Books, 1991.

Hagen, K.L. *Women Respond to the Men's Movement.* New York: HarperCollins, 1992.

Jaggar, Allison M. and Paula S. Rothenberg. *Feminist Frameworks: Alternative Theoretical Accounts of the Relations Between Men and Women.* New York: McGraw-Hill, 1984.

Johnson, Karen. *Trusting Ourselves.* New York: Atlantic Monthly Press, 1990.

Lakoff, R. *Talking Power: The Politics of Language in Our Lives.* New York: Basic Books, 1990.

Learner, Harriet. *The Dance of Anger.* New York: Harper & Row, 1985.

McAllister, Pam. *You Can't Kill the Spirit*. Philadelphia: New Society Publishers, 1988.

Morris, Celia. *Bearing Witness*. Boston: Little Brown, 1994.

Satir, Virginia. *Peoplemaking*. Palo Alto, CA: Science and Behavior Books, 1972.

Smith, Manuel J. *When I Say No I Feel Guilty*. New York: Bantam Books, 1991.

Tannen, Deborah. *You Just Don't Understand: Women and Men in Conversation*. New York: William Morrow, 1990.

Thoele, Sue Patton. *The Courage to Be Yourself*. Berkeley, CA: Conari Press, 1991.

Walmesley, Claire. *Assertiveness: The Right to Be You*. London: BBC Books, 1991.

Zucker, Elaina. *Mastering Assertive Skills*. New York: American Management Association, 1983.

©1994 Whole Person Press 210 W Michigan Duluth MN 55802   (800) 247-6789

Resources

HOW TO USE THIS BOOK

THE EXERCISES

Most of the exercises do not require great expertise. They are practical in various settings: churches, high school or college classrooms, personal growth or human relations laboratories, workshops, or one-time programs such as a Woman's Fair. I have noted the designs which would not be effective in most groups as a one-time/first-time experience. If you belong to an on-going group, you may want to include several experiences from different sections of the book. The order would vary depending upon the nature of the group. Each exercise is based on the following order:

1. Present the topic and its goals.

2. Introduce and guide the activities, providing some structure and also participating in the activities.

3. After the activity, ask participants to examine or apply what they have learned. Most designs include questions for this reflection time.

4. All convene to share what was learned or felt in a plenary session.

5. The exercise is evaluated (if you wish) and group closure takes place.

The time frames indicated in each exercise are only guidelines. Depending upon interest and involvement, a group may take more or less time to complete an activity. The reflection time is very important, not only for its understanding and learning value, but also because it gives participants an opportunity to express any unresolved feelings about the experience. Therefore, allow enough time for reflection—at least as long, if not longer, than the actual experience took. For example, a ten minute activity could have a thirty minute reflection time.

The exercises at the beginning of each section are less threatening and take less skill and experience to conduct. As you begin to use the book, create your own activities or variations of the designs to liven up the process.

THE FORMAT

The format of *Working With Women's Groups, Volume 1,* is designed for easy use. You'll find that each exercise is described completely, including: goals, group size, time frame, materials needed, step-by-step process instructions, and variations.

☞ *Special instructions for the trainer and scripts to be read to the group are typed in italics.*

✔ Questions to ask the group are preceded by a check.

➤ Directions for group activities are indicated by an arrow.

● Mini-lecture notes and sentence-completion fragments are preceded by a bullet.

EXPERIENTIAL LEARNING

Whether acquired in personal life or in the group, learning is likely to follow a certain pattern. Group theorists have set up variations of what is basically one model. The model used in this book includes the following four steps:

Step 1 - Experience

The activity itself or anything that happens within a group.

Step 2 - Identify

Separating out a specific portion of the data which the group would like to understand. Questions that may help are:

✔ What experience shall we look at?

✔ What messages should we explore?

✔ What behavior shall we work on?

✔ Does everyone recall when that happened?

Step 3 - Analyze

Focusing on thoughts and feelings about the identified behavior. Moving deeper into reasons behind the data—causes and effects that deepen the understanding of the chosen behavior. Questions that may help are:

✔ What were your reactions?

✔ What were your feelings and thoughts?

✔ What were the possible reasons for your reactions in this situation? (Do not ask "why" questions which tend to probe inner motivations and elicit defensiveness.)

✔ Was what happened a help or a hindrance?

✔ To whom?

✔ What does this mean?

©1994 Whole Person Press 210 W Michigan Duluth MN 55802   (800) 247-6789

Step 4 - Generalize and Apply

Learning takes place at this step, where conclusions are drawn, hypotheses are made, and participants are ready to move toward future action now that some understanding has occurred. Questions that may help are:

✔ Based on what we have said and heard, what conclusions can we draw?

✔ What might we have done instead of . . . ?

✔ How could we apply what we have been discussing to other situations?

This model is experiential—it starts with the experience, the activity in the group, and anything that happens or is discussed in the group. Then reflection, which requires some discipline, must follow. Learning is not likely to happen without it.

FACILITATING THE DESIGNS

The exercises in this book propose learning in groups. Some can be useful to individual readers. Learning groups are generally more effective with facilitators. Facilitators, however, are not experts with all the answers, but rather persons who participate in the groups, as well as provide some structure and group skills. A key principle is that someone who has experienced something is more expert in it than the experts.

As the group develops, members other than the designated facilitators will, and should, be encouraged to fill facilitation functions, e.g., suggesting directions, sharing observations, clarifying and summarizing what is said, and initiating ideas. Effective facilitators do not give answers and/or advice, nor do they tell members what they should have learned. They do listen, question, clarify, and in general help members understand what they are saying and learning. They do not set themselves up as the primary source of acceptance and support in the group; rather they encourage group members to support and accept each other. Facilitators also can keep members from digressing. Competent facilitators will be active in a group, yet not monopolize or keep others from participating. They can make certain that the group does not devote too much time to one person. Everyone should have time to share and really be heard.

In summary, a facilitator helps the group to get started, to build trust, to create a learning atmosphere. She also proposes and manages the designs, assists the group members to reach deeper levels of sharing, encourages each woman to make her own decisions, and shares herself. This type of facilitation enables women to move from other-approved and other-directed lives to self-approval, self-direction, and finally self-support.

It is best when persons who act as facilitators or leaders for the exercises in this book possess most of the following qualities:

1. Some understanding of group processes—how groups develop, what issues may emerge, etc.

2. Motivation to be part of the group, with expectations of enjoying and learning from each session.

3. Flexibility in conducting the learning designs—looking to women in each group to help provide input for the designs and direction to be taken since each group varies in wants, interests, and resources.

4. Positive self-regard and some understanding of self, having spent time working on her own issues and yet also committed to her continued self growth.

5. Understanding of how her own behavior often affects others.

6. Knowledge of what she hopes will happen when she intervenes in the group and knowledge of her reasons for the intervention.

7. Ability to support and confront other women in a way that they can hear without becoming defensive.

8. Enough awareness of self so that she knows when she is not able to perceive clearly what is happening or when she is getting "hooked."

9. Ability to empathize with other women—hearing what they are saying and feeling, sensing where they may be when they come to the group.

10. Respect for diversity and acceptance of differing styles of group members—allowing all members the freedom to participate in their own way and at their own pace (and intervening if any members appear to be experiencing pressure from other group members).

11. Willingness to explore her own racism, classicism, heterosexism, or any other "isms" as they apply.

12. Ease in establishing an informal, warm, supportive atmosphere—a relaxed approach.

13. Ability to encourage experimentation and the trying out of new behavior in the group.

There is value in having two facilitators in each group. An effective ratio of participants to facilitators is two facilitators for a group of eight to ten. This allows for greater participation (e.g., one can work on a personal issue while the other stays on top of the group process). It is also a positive collaborative model of women in teamwork. Also, each facilitator brings different resources with her which can enhance the group's experience.

In the first session, the facilitators should inform the group of their perception of their role and how they want to function; asking for the group's input, and working out differing perceptions of the facilitation role.

If you are without prior experience in group leadership and this sounds difficult, don't be discouraged. Assess your skills generously. It's likely you can handle the facilitating roles, especially if you keep in mind that not all the structured activities require experienced facilitators. Teachers, for example, can use many of these designs in the classroom. They already know their group, and the activities are self-explanatory to a degree. Many voluntary women's organizations, church congregations, and the like have members with the necessary skill, levelheadedness, and courage to facilitate learning groups.

Regardless of your level of experience and skills, do not try an activity out in a group if you feel uncomfortable about it. Use the book selectively, trusting your own feelings about the activities suggested. Understand the exercise well before conducting it in a group. If possible, try out the activity on yourself first. This gives you time to clear up any directions and get some idea of the feelings and issues the activity will raise.

GROUP GUIDELINES

It is helpful in the beginning of a new group or workshop for the facilitators to involve the members in a discussion about group norms. This alleviates part of the members' anxiety of not knowing what to expect or what the rules are to be in the group. A facilitator may wish to share some items that are non-negotiable. It is critical that members feel commitment and accountability for the guidelines agreed upon. Some suggested guidelines are as follows:

1. Regular attendance.

2. Mutual confidentiality: you may share your own experiences, but do not discuss what another person said or did in any way that others may be able to identify her.

3. Active participation, although participation in any given activity is voluntary. And no one dominates.

4. Start on time and end on time.

5. Make personal statements, and use "I" messages (not, "we all are feeling bored," rather, "I am feeling bored").

6. If you have something to say to a person talk to them directly (not, "I find Susan to be an intelligent woman," instead, "Susan, I think you are very intelligent, especially the way you are able to . . . ").

7. Share your feelings and thoughts honestly.

8. Respect diversity.

9. Take responsibility for yourself and your feelings. If you are feeling upset by what is happening in the group, share this feeling and try to change what the group is doing.

10. Don't moralize or give advice. Instead, clarify options and make suggestions.

EVALUATION

Evaluation of an exercise is at the discretion of the facilitator. Therefore I have not included evaluation suggestions with most of the exercises. Facilitators will receive informal feedback from participants. It takes forms such as how interested, excited, or involved members seem to be; what members say after the meeting to the facilitator, to each other, and to outsiders; and whether they do or do not come back again. However, the feedback may not be clear unless there is a more formal evaluation process. Reasons for success or failure in the group can help you know what to include or change the next time. Some possible areas to examine:

1. Were the goals of the exercise/workshop achieved?

2. Were the personal goals of the participants achieved?

3. What was learned?

4. What new skills were gained?

5. What did the facilitators do that was helpful/unhelpful?

6. What are participants feeling about the experience?

7. Which activities and parts of the workshop session were most helpful and the least helpful?

8. How do participants feel about group communication or climate?

9. What future learning and growth opportunities would members like to see offered?

There are a variety of ways to obtain this information:

1. Stop the action in the group and ask: "How is everyone feeling right now?"

2. Pass around written forms to be completed by the participants.

3. Invite participants to respond verbally to questions: e.g., "What did you learn from today's session?"

4. Write a scale on an easel chart and instruct members to go up and check where they are, for example:

Level of Satisfaction with Session

Low 1 2 3 4 5 6 7 8 9 10 High

5. Ask participants for a word that expresses how they are feeling about the session.

6. As facilitator, make your own observations about how the members' self-esteem seems to be changing, growing, and increasing.

THE LEARNING ENVIRONMENT

The group setting has an impact on how groups function. The most effective setting for a group is a small or a medium size room with a comfortable rug, cushions to sit on, and comfortable chairs, plus a black board or walls on which to hang easel sheets. Refreshments should be available.

The room should be a quiet place where no one else will intrude. If child care is provided during the sessions, the children need to be far enough away that they cannot be heard. It also helps one's sense of privacy and freedom to have the group meet in a room where the group's laughing, crying, or singing does not disturb others.

Group members should generally be encouraged to sit in a circle. This is the most effective setting since it provides for easier verbal and nonverbal communication and offers an atmosphere of inclusion.

If members come and go, be sure to allow women to leave in a positive way and make sure to include new members.

Do not start a group unless there are seven or more participants. With fewer, the experience may become more intense than intended. Eight to fifteen persons in a group plus facilitators will allow an ideal variety of perceptions, attitudes, etc. Keep members in the same small group for most of the work time if it is an on-going group. Thus, trust and support can build.

GROUP PUBLICITY

How and where the group is publicized will affect how many women sign up. Some effective techniques are to:

➤ Design an attractive flier about the event.

➤ Send the flier or make phone calls to friends, women activists, and prominent women; invite and ask them to tell others about the group experience.

> Place an announcement in local newspapers, on radio and/or television, as well as in the newsletters of women's organizations or on prominent bulletin boards, in church foyers, and storefronts.

> Invite one or several women's organizations or colleges to co-sponsor the group.

The best publicity is women who have had a positive experience in a previous group.

GROUP PREPARATIONS

The facilitators should meet before the first session for their own team building—to talk about what expectations, investments, and goals each has for the group. Take some time to get to know each other better. Then choose the exercises for the group, discuss the specific activities, try them out, and assign roles to each facilitator.

Send a letter of acceptance to women who register for a group or telephone them personally. Some things to include are:

1. Welcome!
2. Place, date, times.
3. What to wear and bring.
4. Purpose of the group.
5. Contact person.

Along with the letter, you may want to include an advance information questionnaire which gives some idea who is coming and what their expectations are. A sample follows (see next page).

ADVANCE INFORMATION QUESTIONNAIRE
(*Title of the Group/Workshop*)

We would like the following information about you in order to help us design the (*name of group*) in line with your expectations.

Name:

Age:

Occupation:

How did you learn about this experience?

What are your expectations of the (*name of group*)? What do you want to happen?

What do you want to get out of the (*name of group*) for yourself? When you leave the group, what awarenesses, skills, feelings, values, etc. would you like to take with you?

What are your feelings right now about coming?

Any other information you would like us to have . . .

Please return this paper with your information by: (date)
To: (return address)

WHOLE PERSON ASSOCIATES RESOURCES

Our materials are designed to address the whole person—physical, emotional, mental, spiritual, and social. Developed for trainers by trainers, all of these resources are ready-to-use. Novice trainers will find everything they need to get started, and the expert trainer will discover new ideas and concepts to add to their existing programs.

GROUP PROCESS RESOURCES

All of the exercises in our group process resources encourage interaction between the leader and participants, as well as among the participants. Each exercise includes everything you need to present a meaningful program: goals, optimal group size, time frame, materials list, and the complete process instructions.

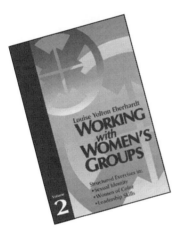

WORKING WITH WOMEN'S GROUPS
Volume 2
Louise Yolton Eberhardt

The second volume of **Working with Women's Groups** has been completely revised and updated. These exercises will help women explore issues that are of perennial concern as well as today's hot topics.

Volume 2 topics include:
- sexuality issues
- women of color
- leadership skills training

WORKING WITH WOMEN'S GROUPS
WORKSHEET MASTERS

Complete packages of full-size (8 1/2" x 11") photocopy masters that include all the worksheets and handouts from **Working with Women's Groups volume 1 and 2** are available to you. Use the masters for easy duplication of the handouts for each participant.

- ❏ **WG1 / Working with Women's Groups—Volume 1 / $24.95**
- ❏ **WG2 / Working with Women's Groups—Volume 2 / $24.95**
- ❏ **WG1W / Working with Women's Groups—Volume 1 Worksheet Masters / $9.95**
- ❏ **WG2W / Working with Women's Groups—Volume 2 Worksheet Masters / $9.95**

©1994 Whole Person Press 210 W Michigan Duluth MN 55802   (800) 247-6789

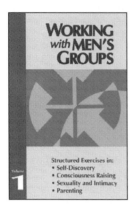

WORKING WITH MEN'S GROUPS

Roger Karsk and Bill Thomas

Also revised and updated, this volume is a valuable resource for anyone working with men's groups. The exercises cover a variety of topics, including:

- self discovery
- parenting
- conflict
- intimacy

❑ **MG / Working with Men's Groups / $24.95**
❑ **MGW / Working with Men's Groups
   Worksheet Masters / $9.95**

WORKING WITH GROUPS FROM
DYSFUNCTIONAL FAMILIES

Cheryl Hetherington

This collection of 29 proven group activities is designed to heal the pain that results from growing up in or living in a dysfunctional family. With these exercises you can:

- promote healing
- build self-esteem
- encourage sharing
- help participants acknowledge their feelings

WORKING WITH GROUPS FROM DYSFUNCTIONAL FAMILIES
REPRODUCIBLE WORKSHEET MASTERS

A complete package of full-size (8 1/2" x 11") photocopy masters that include all the worksheets and handouts from **Working with Groups from Dysfunctional Families** is available to you. Use the masters for easy duplication of the handouts for each participant.

❑ **DFH / Working with Groups from Dysfunctional Families / $24.95**
❑ **DFW / Dysfunctional Families Worksheet Masters / $9.95**

©1994 Whole Person Press 210 W Michigan Duluth MN 55802   (800) 247-6789

WELLNESS ACTIVITIES FOR YOUTH
Volumes 1 & 2
Sandy Queen

Each volume of **Wellness Activities
for Youth** helps leaders teach children
and teenagers about wellness with
a whole person approach, a "no
put-down" rule, and most of all,
an emphasis on FUN. The
concepts include:

- values
- stress and coping
- self-esteem
- personal well-being
- social wellness

WELLNESS ACTIVITIES FOR YOUTH
WORKSHEET MASTERS

Complete packages of full-size (8 1/2" x 11") photocopy masters that include
all the worksheets and handouts from **Wellness Activities for Youth Volumes 1 and 2** are available to you. Use the masters for easy duplication of
the handouts for each participant.

- ❏ **WY1 / Wellness Activities for Youth Volume 1 / $19.95**
- ❏ **WY2 / Wellness Activities for Youth Volume 2 / $19.95**
- ❏ **WY1W / Wellness Activities for Youth V. 1 Worksheet Masters / $9.95**
- ❏ **WY2W / Wellness Activities for Youth V. 2 Worksheet Masters / $9.95**

PLAYFUL ACTIVITIES FOR
POWERFUL PRESENTATIONS
Bruce Williamson

This book contains 40 fun exercises designed to fit
any group or topic. These exercises will help you:

- build teamwork
- encourage laughter and playfulness
- relieve stress and tension
- free up the imaginations of participants

- ❏ **PAP / Playful Activities for Powerful Presentations
  $19.95**

©1994 Whole Person Press 210 W Michigan Duluth MN 55802   (800) 247-6789

STRUCTURED EXERCISES
IN STRESS MANAGEMENT—VOLUMES 1-4

Nancy Loving Tubesing, EdD and Donald A. Tubesing, PhD, Editors

Each book in this four-volume series contains 36 ready-to-use teaching modules that involve the participant—as a whole person—in learning how to manage stress more effectively.

Each exercise is carefully designed by top stress-management professionals. Instructions are clearly written and field-tested so that even beginning trainers can smoothly lead a group through warm-up and closure, reflection and planning, and action and interaction—all with minimum preparation time.

Each Stress Handbook is brimming with practical ideas that you can weave into your own teaching designs or mix and match to develop new programs for varied settings, audiences, and time frames. In each volume you'll find **Icebreakers, Stress Assessments, Management Strategies, Skill Builders, Action Planners, Closing Processes** and **Group Energizers**—all with a special focus on stress management.

STRUCTURED EXERCISES
IN WELLNESS PROMOTION—VOLUMES 1-4

Nancy Loving Tubesing, EdD and Donald A. Tubesing, PhD, Editors

Discover the Wellness Handbooks—from the wellness pioneers at Whole Person Associates. Each volume in this innovative series includes 36 experiential learning activities that focus on whole person health—body, mind, spirit, emotions, relationships, and lifestyle.

The exercises, developed by an interdisciplinary pool of leaders in the wellness movement nationwide, actively encourage people to adopt wellness-oriented attitudes and to develop more responsible self-care patterns.

All process designs in the Wellness Handbooks are clearly explained and have been thoroughly field-tested with diverse audiences so that trainers can use them with confidence. **Icebreakers, Wellness Explorations, Self-Care Strategies, Action Planners, Closings** and **Group Energizers** are all ready-to-go—including reproducible worksheets, scripts, and chalktalk outlines—for the busy professional who wants to develop unique wellness programs without spending oodles of time in preparation.

©1994 Whole Person Press 210 W Michigan Duluth MN 55802   (800) 247-6789

STRUCTURED EXERCISES IN STRESS AND WELLNESS ARE AVAILABLE IN TWO FORMATS

LOOSE-LEAF FORMAT (8 1/2" x 11")

The loose-leaf, 3-ring binder format provides you with maximum flexiblity. The binder gives you plenty of room to add your own adaptations, workshop outlines, or notes right where you need them. The index tabs offer quick and easy access to each section of exercises, and the generous margins allow plenty of room for notes. In addition an extra set of the full-size worksheets and handouts are packaged separately for convenient duplication.

SOFTCOVER FORMAT (6" x 9")

The softcover format is a perfect companion to the loose-leaf version. This smaller book fits easily into your briefcase or bag, and the binding has been designed to remain open on your desk or lecturn. Worksheets and handouts can be enlarged and photocopied for distribution to your participants, or you can purchase sets of worksheet masters.

WORKSHEET MASTERS

The Worksheet Masters for the two Structured Exercise series offer full-size (8 1/2" x 11") photocopy masters. All of the worksheets and handouts for each volume are reproduced in easy-to-read print with professional graphics. All you need to do to complete your workshop preparation is run them through a copier.

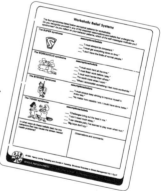

Structured Exercises in Stress Management

    ❏ **Loose-Leaf Edition—Volume 1-4 / $54.95 each**
    ❏ **Softcover Edition—Volume 1-4 / $29.95 each**
    ❏ **Worksheet Masters—Volume 1-4 / $9.95 each**

Structured Exercises in Wellness Promotion

    ❏ **Loose-Leaf Edition—Volume 1-4 / $54.95 each**
    ❏ **Softcover Edition—Volume 1-4 / $29.95 each**
    ❏ **Worksheet Masters—Volume 1-4 / $9.95 each**

©1994 Whole Person Press 210 W Michigan Duluth MN 55802   (800) 247-6789

WORKSHOPS-IN-A-BOOK

KICKING YOUR STRESS HABITS:
A Do-it-yourself Guide to Coping with Stress
Donald A. Tubesing, PhD

Over a quarter of a million people have found ways to deal with their everyday stress by using **Kicking Your Stress Habits**. This workshop-in-a-book actively involves the reader in assessing stressful patterns and developing more effective coping strategies with helpful "Stop and Reflect" sections in each chapter.

The 10-step planning process and 20 skills for managing stress make **Kicking Your Stress Habits** an ideal text for stress management classes in many different settings, from hospitals to universities and for a wide variety of groups.

❑ K / Kicking Your Stress Habits / 14.95

SEEKING YOUR HEALTHY BALANCE:
A Do-it-yourself Guide to Whole Person Well-being
Donald A. Tubesing, PhD and Nancy Loving Tubesing, EdD

Where can you find the time and energy to "do it all" without sacrificing your health and well-being? **Seeking Your Healthy Balance** helps the reader discover how to make changes toward a more balanced lifestyle by learning effective ways to juggle work, self, and others; clarifying self-care options; and discovering and setting their own personal priorities.

Seeking Your Healthy Balance asks the questions and helps readers find their own answers.

❑ HB / Seeking Your Healthy Balance / 14.95

©1994 Whole Person Press 210 W Michigan Duluth MN 55802   (800) 247-6789

RELAXATION RESOURCES

Many trainers and workshop leaders have discovered the benefits of relaxation and visualization in healing the body, mind, and spirit.

30 SCRIPTS FOR RELAXATION, IMAGERY, AND INNER HEALING
Julie Lusk

These two volumes are collections of relaxation scripts created by trainers for trainers. The 30 scripts in each of the two volumes have been professionally-tested and fine-tuned so they are ready to use for both novice and expert trainers.

Help your participants change their behavior, enhance their self-esteem, discover inner, private places, and heal themselves through simple trainer-led guided imagery scripts. Both volumes include information on how to use the scripts, suggestions for tailoring them to your specific needs and audience, and information on how to successfully incorporate guided imagery into your existing programs.

❑ 30S / 30 Scripts for Relaxation, Imagery, and Inner Healing—Volume 1 / $19.95
❑ 30S2 / 30 Scripts for Relaxation, Imagery, and Inner Healing—Volume 2 / $19.95

INQUIRE WITHIN
Andrew Schwartz

Use visualization to make positive changes in your life. The 24 visualization experiences in **Inquire Within** will help participants enhance their creativity, heal inner pain, learn to relax, and deal with conflict. Each visualization includes questions at the end of the process that encourage deeper reflection and a better understanding of the exercise and the response it invokes.

❑ IW / Inquire Within / $19.95

RELAXATION AUDIOTAPES

Perhaps you're an old hand at relaxation, looking for new ideas. Or maybe you're a beginner, just testing the waters. Whatever your relaxation needs, Whole Person tapes provide a whole family of techniques for reducing physical and mental stress. To assist in your decision-making, you may want to know more about different types of relaxation.

We offer six different types of relaxation techniques in our twenty-one tapes. The Whole Person series ranges from simple breathing and stretching exercises, to classic autogenic and progressive relaxation sequences, to guided meditations and whimsical daydreams. All are carefully crafted to promote whole person relaxation—body, mind, and spirit. We also provide a line of music-only tapes, composed specifically for relaxation.

SENSATIONAL RELAXATION

When stress piles up, it becomes a heavy load both physically and emotionally. These full-length relaxation experiences will teach you techniques that can be used whenever you feel that stress is getting out of control. Choose one you like and repeat it daily until it becomes second nature then recall that technique whenever you need it.

- ❑ **CD / Countdown to Relaxation / $9.95**
- ❑ **DS / Daybreak / Sundown / $9.95**
- ❑ **TDB / Take a Deep Breath / $9.95**
- ❑ **RLX / Relax . . . Let Go . . . Relax / $9.95**
- ❑ **SRL / StressRelease / $9.95**
- ❑ **WRM / Warm and Heavy / $9.95**

STRESS BREAKS

Do you need a short energy booster or a quick stress reliever? If you don't know what type of relaxation you like, or if you are new to guided relaxation techniques, try one of our Stress Breaks for a quick refocusing or change of pace any time of the day.

- ❑ **BT / BreakTime / $9.95**
- ❑ **NT / Natural Tranquilizers / $9.95**

DAYDREAMS

Escape from the stress around you with guided tours to beautiful places. Picture yourself traveling to the ocean, sitting in a park, luxuriating in the view from the majestic mountains, or enjoying the solitude and serenity of a cozy cabin. The 10-minute escapes included in our Daydream tapes will lead your imagination away from your everyday cares so you can resume your tasks relaxed and comforted.

❑ **DD1 / Daydreams 1: Getaways / $9.95**
❑ **DD2 / Daydreams 2: Peaceful Places / $9.95**

GUIDED MEDITATION

Take a step beyond relaxation and discover the connection between body and mind with guided meditation. The imagery in our full-length meditations will help you discover your strengths, find healing, make positive life changes, and recognize your inner wisdom.

❑ **IH / Inner Healing / $9.95**
❑ **PE / Personal Empowering / $9.95**
❑ **HBT / Healthy Balancing / $9.95**
❑ **SPC / Spiritual Centering / $9.95**

WILDERNESS DAYDREAMS

Discover the healing power of nature with the four tapes in the Wilderness Daydreams series. The eight special journeys will transport you from your harried, stressful surroundings to the peaceful serenity of words and water.

❑ **WD1 / Canoe / Rain / $9.95**
❑ **WD2 / Island /Spring / $9.95**
❑ **WD3 / Campfire / Stream / $9.95**
❑ **WD4 / Sailboat / Pond / $9.95**

MUSIC ONLY

No relaxation program would be complete without relaxing melodies that can be played as background to a prepared script or that can be enjoyed as you practice a technique you have already learned. Steven Eckels composed his melodies specifically for relaxation. These "musical prayers for healing" will calm your body, mind, and spirit.

❑ **T / Tranquility / $9.95**
❑ **H / Harmony / $9.95**
❑ **S / Serenity / $9.95**

Titles can be combined for discounts!

QUANTITY DISCOUNT			
1 - 9	10 - 49	50 - 99	100+
$9.95	$8.95	$7.96	CALL

©1994 Whole Person Press 210 W Michigan Duluth MN 55802   (800) 247-6789

ORDER FORM

Name _____

Address _____

City _____

State/Zip _____

Area Code/Telephone _____

Please make checks payable to:
Whole Person Associates Inc
210 West Michigan
Duluth MN 55802-1908
FAX: 1-218-727-0505
TOLL FREE: 1-800-247-6789

Books / Workshops-In-A-Book

___ Kicking Your Stress Habits .... $14.95 _____

___ Seeking Your Healthy Balance .... $14.95 _____

Structured Exercises in Stress Management Series—Volumes 1-4

___ Stress Softcover Edition .... Vol 1 ___ Vol 2 ___ Vol 3 ___ Vol 4 ___ $29.95 _____

___ Stress Loose-Leaf Edition .... Vol 1 ___ Vol 2 ___ Vol 3 ___ Vol 4 ___ $54.95 _____

___ Stress Worksheet Masters .... Vol 1 ___ Vol 2 ___ Vol 3 ___ Vol 4 ___ $9.95 _____

Structured Exercises in Wellness Promotion Series—Volumes 1-4

___ Wellness Softcover Edition .... Vol 1 ___ Vol 2 ___ Vol 3 ___ Vol 4 ___ $29.95 _____

___ Wellness Loose-Leaf Edition .... Vol 1 ___ Vol 2 ___ Vol 3 ___ Vol 4 ___ $54.95 _____

___ Wellness Worksheet Masters .... Vol 1 ___ Vol 2 ___ Vol 3 ___ Vol 4 ___ $9.95 _____

Group Process Resources

___ Playful Activities for Powerful Presentations .... $19.95 _____

___ Working with Groups from Dysfunctional Families .... $24.95 _____

___ Working with Groups from Dysfunctional Families Worksheet Masters .... $9.95 _____

___ Working with Women's Groups .... Vol 1 ___ Vol 2 ___ $24.95 _____

___ Working with Women's Groups Worksheet Masters .... Vol 1 ___ Vol 2 ___ $9.95 _____

___ Working with Men's Groups .... $24.95 _____

___ Working with Men's Groups Worksheet Masters .... $9.95 _____

___ Wellness Activities for Youth .... Vol 1 ___ Vol 2 ___ $19.95 _____

___ Wellness Activities for Youth Worksheet Masters .... Vol 1 ___ Vol 2 ___ $9.95 _____

Relaxation Audiotapes

___ BreakTime .... $ 9.95 _____

___ Countdown to Relaxation .... $ 9.95 _____

___ Daybreak/Sundown .... $ 9.95 _____

___ Daydreams 1: Getaways .... $ 9.95 _____

___ Daydreams 2: Peaceful Places .... $ 9.95 _____

___ Harmony (music only) .... $ 9.95 _____

___ Healthy Balancing .... $ 9.95 _____

___ Inner Healing .... $ 9.95 _____

___ Natural Tranquilizers .... $ 9.95 _____

___ Personal Empowering .... $ 9.95 _____

___ Relax . . . Let Go . . . Relax .... $ 9.95 _____

___ Serenity (music only) .... $ 9.95 _____

___ Spiritual Centering .... $ 9.95 _____

___ StressRelease .... $ 9.95 _____

___ Take a Deep Breath .... $ 9.95 _____

___ Tranquility (music only) .... $ 9.95 _____

___ Warm and Heavy .... $ 9.95 _____

___ Wilderness DD 1: Canoe/Rain .... $ 9.95 _____

___ Wilderness DD 2: Island/Spring .... $ 9.95 _____

___ Wilderness DD 3: Campfire/Stream .... $ 9.95 _____

___ Wilderness DD 4: Sailboat/Pond .... $ 9.95 _____

Relaxation Resources

___ 30 Scripts—Volume 1 .... $19.95 _____

___ 30 Scripts—Volume 2 .... $19.95 _____

___ Inquire Within .... $19.95 _____

My check is enclosed. **(US funds only)**

Please charge my_____Visa _____Mastercard

_____

Exp date _____

Signature _____

SUBTOTAL _____
TAX (MN residents 6.5%) _____
7% GST-Canadian customers only _____
**SHIPPING* _____
GRAND TOTAL _____

** **SHIPPING**. $5.00 ($8.00 outside U.S.)
Please call us for quotes on UPS 3rd Day,
2nd Day or Next Day Air.

About Whole Person Associates

At Whole Person Associates, we're 100% committed to providing stress and wellness materials that involve participants and have a "whole person" focus—body, mind, spirit, and relationships.

That's our mission and it's very important to us—but it doesn't tell the whole story. Behind the products in our catalog is a company full of people—and *that's* what really makes us who we are.

ABOUT THE OWNERS

Whole Person Associates was created by the vision of two people: Donald A. Tubesing, PhD, and Nancy Loving Tubesing, EdD. Since way back in 1970, Don and Nancy have been active in the stress management/wellness promotion movement—consulting, leading seminars, writing, and publishing. Most of our early products were the result of their creativity and expertise.

Living proof that you can "stay evergreen," Don and Nancy remain the driving force behind the company and are still very active in developing new products that touch people's lives.

ABOUT THE COMPANY

Whole Person Associates was "born" in Duluth, Minnesota, and we remain committed to our lovely city on the shore of Lake Superior. All of our operations are here, which makes communication between departments much easier! We've grown since our beginnings, but at a steady pace—we're interested in sustainable growth that allows us to keep our down-to-earth orientation.

We put the same high quality into every product we offer, translating the best of current research into practical, accessible, easy-to-use materials. In this way we can create the best possible resources to help our customers teach about stress management and wellness promotion.

We also strive to treat our customers as we would like to be treated. If we fall short of our goals in any way, please let us know.

ABOUT OUR EMPLOYEES

Speaking of down-to-earth, that's a requirement for each and every one of our employees. We're all product consultants, which means that anyone who answers the phone can probably answer your questions (if they can't, they'll find someone who can.)

We focus on helping you find the products that fit your needs. And we've found that the best way to do that is to hire friendly and resourceful people.

ABOUT OUR ASSOCIATES

Who are the "associates" in Whole Person Associates? They're the trainers, authors, musicians, and others who have developed much of the material you see on these pages. We're always on the lookout for high-quality products that reflect our "whole person" philosophy and fill a need for our customers.

Most of our products were developed by experts who are the tops in their fields, and we're very proud to be associated with them.

ABOUT OUR CUSTOMERS

Finally, we wouldn't have a reason to exist without you, our customers. We've met some of you, and we've talked to many more of you on the phone. We are always aware that without you, there would be no Whole Person Associates.

That's why we'd love to hear from you! Let us know what you think of our products—how you use them in your work, what additional products you'd like to see, and what shortcomings you've noted. Write us or call on our toll-free line. We look forward to hearing from you!

©1994 Whole Person Press 210 W Michigan Duluth MN 55802   (800) 247-6789